I0169529

# Luke

# Dwelling in God's Word

# Luke

The Humble Blessed, the Proud Brought Low:
A Fifty-Day Devotional

## GRAHAM JOSEPH HILL

Eagna Publishing • Sydney, Australia

LUKE

The Humble Blessed, the Proud Brought Low: A Fifty-Day Devotional

Copyright © 2025 Graham Joseph Hill. All rights reserved. Except for brief quotations in critical publications or reviews, no part of this book may be reproduced in any manner without prior written permission from the publisher. Scripture quotations are from the New International Version, unless noted otherwise. Used by permission.

Published by: Eagna Publishing (Sydney, Australia)
eagnapublishing@icloud.com
Cover and interior design: Graham Joseph Hill

paperback isbn: 978-1-7641791-0-2
ebook isbn: 978-1-7641791-1-9
version number 2025-10-24

**NATIONAL LIBRARY OF AUSTRALIA**

A catalogue record for this book is available from the National Library of Australia

IV

# Contents

# Introduction

This devotional is part of a larger pilgrimage through Scripture, shepherded by Rev. Dr. Graham Joseph Hill, as he walks with readers from Genesis to Revelation. The Dwelling in God's Word series (both podcast and written reflections) invites you to discover how each book of the Bible speaks to the deep longings of the soul and the demands of our shared life in the world. It's not merely a reading plan; it's a sacred journey of formation and transformation. Here, the biblical narrative meets everyday discipleship in prayerful and practical ways.

The Gospel of Luke sings with breadth, beauty, and spiritual longing. It's a Gospel written for wanderers and questioners, for the marginalized and the powerful, for those aching for justice, and for those clinging to hope. Luke integrates history, theology, and story remarkably, revealing the compassionate face of God made flesh. Here, Jesus doesn't just announce the kingdom of God; he embodies it in table fellowship, in healing touch, in parables of lost sons and found grace.

Luke's Jesus is always moving toward the outsider. This Gospel is steeped in reversal, where the low are lifted, the proud are scattered, and the hungry are filled. It's a Gospel of songs: Mary's Magnificat, Zechariah's prophecy, Simeon's cry, and the angels' chorus. It sings of salvation not as an escape but as God's deep entry into the wounds and wonder of the world.

From dusty roads to upper rooms, Luke invites us into a faith that thinks, weeps and walks. It's a Gospel of prayer and the Spirit, of storytelling and justice. And at the center of it all is Jesus, the friend of sinners, the suffering prophet, and the risen Lord, whose mercy is always moving ahead of us, calling us into the life of the kingdom.

This devotional is rooted in the richness of the biblical text and nourished by careful theological reflection. It invites you to sit with Scripture: slowly, reverently, attentively. Each entry draws you deeper into Luke's Gospel, exposing overlooked treasures and summoning fresh faith. But this isn't just about knowing more. It's about living differently. As you journey through these pages, you'll be challenged to embrace justice, embody mercy, cultivate humility, and become a participant in the reconciling mission of God.

These reflections don't avoid hard questions or flatten the text into sentiment. They dare to wrestle. To pray. To imagine. And they call you to more than contemplation. They invite you to action: to live the Gospel in your neighborhood, your body, your workplace, your church.

As you immerse yourself in this devotional, may your theology deepen, your heart soften, and your hands be ready to serve. May these fifty days in Luke stir something courageous in you: a longing to see and be seen by the living Christ.

How to Use This Devotional:
1. This book leads you through the Gospel of Luke in fifty short devotions.
2. You're encouraged to pair this with the companion podcast: https://grahamjosephhill.com/devotions.
3. Each day, you're invited to:
a. Read the passage slowly, letting it read you.
b. Sit with the day's devotion and let its truths sink deep.
c. Pray, honestly and vulnerably, into the text.
d. Discern one concrete action in response.

Whether you read alone, with family, or within a community, this journey through Luke will shape your heart and stretch your faith. Come ready to be changed.

# Day 1: Trusting God's Surprising Way

## Reading: Luke 1:1–38

Our modern age likes to give us the impression that we are masters of our destinies and shapers of history. Our cultures praise human effort, creativity, and will. How many organizations have vision statements, and people fill diaries with purposes and plans? But time and again, the Scriptures remind us that God controls our lives and human history. God rules and reigns over lives, nations, history, and the cosmos and often breaks into human lives unexpectedly and miraculously.

In this passage, we're introduced to two miraculous announcements. The angel Gabriel first appears to Zechariah, proclaiming the birth of John the Baptist, and then to Mary, announcing the birth of Jesus. These encounters, filled with divine mystery and God's glorious plans, invite us into a space of reflection on God's surprising ways.

When Luke recounts the foretelling of the birth of John the Baptist, Luke goes to great lengths to show the righteousness of Zechariah and Elizabeth. But their righteousness didn't protect them from loss and pain. "Both of them were righteous in the sight of God, observing all the Lord's commands and decrees blamelessly. But they were childless because Elizabeth could not conceive, and they were both very old" (Luke 1:6–7). Although Zechariah is religious, he's shocked when the angel Gabriel appears to him. Who would blame him? Though

3

he initially doubts the angel's words, God promises Zechariah a son who will prepare the way for the Messiah.

It's fascinating that the people of faith are in this story of the two women, Elizabeth and Mary, John the Baptist's and Jesus Christ's mothers. When Elizabeth falls pregnant with John, she proclaims, "The Lord has done this for me. In these days he has shown his favor and taken away my disgrace among the people" (Luke 1:25). Elizabeth celebrates God's power, will, and compassion. Similarly, when the angel foretells the birth of Jesus, Mary responds with faith and surrender despite the unimaginable news that she, a virgin, will conceive the Son of God. Her words, "I am the Lord's servant. May your word to me be fulfilled," echo a profound trust in God's plan (Luke 1:38).

These stories leading up to the birth of John the Baptist and Jesus Christ remind us that God often works through the unexpected, inviting us to embrace the divine will with open hearts. Zechariah's initial doubt, Elizabeth's celebration of God's favor and compassion, and Mary's humble, faith-filled acceptance lead to fulfilling God's promises. The Spirit of God invites us into a similar trust and surrender, even when God's plans seem beyond our understanding. As we reflect on these announcements, we can ask for the grace to respond with Mary's faith, Elizabeth's delight, and Zechariah's eventual joy, trusting that God's ways, though mysterious and surprising, are always woven with love and purpose.

This passage also points to Jesus Christ, honoring the divine presence and purpose in his birth and nature. Jesus fulfills God's promises and covenant, is the Messiah promised in the Hebrew Scriptures, and will reign forever. The angel tells Mary, "You will conceive and give birth to a son, and you are to call him Jesus. He will be great and will be called the Son of the Most High. The Lord God will give him the throne of his father David, and he will reign over Jacob's descendants forever; his kingdom will never end" (Luke 1:31–33).

4

**Guiding Truth:** God's unexpected plans invite us to trust and surrender to God's loving and purposeful will and guidance.

**Reflection:** How can I cultivate a heart that trusts in God's plans, even when they seem beyond my understanding? In what ways can I celebrate and embrace the unexpected ways God works in my life?

**Prayer:** Lord God, your ways often surprise and challenge us. Grant us the faith of Mary, the hope of Elizabeth, and the eventual joy of Zechariah. Please help us trust your divine plans, even when they seem beyond our understanding. May we surrender our doubts and embrace your will with open hearts, knowing that your love guides everything. Amen.

# Day 2: Songs of Radical Faith

## Reading: Luke 1:39–80

The songs of Mary and Zechariah are profound and prophetic. Mary glorifies God, recognizes God's compassion toward her, praises the power of God to bring down rulers and lift the humble, proclaims God's concern for the hungry instead of the powerful and wealthy, and tells of God's faithfulness in keeping promises to Israel. Zechariah praises God for fulfilling the divine promises to Israel, prophecies that God is raising a Savior from the house of David as promised. Zechariah proclaims John's role in preparing the way for the saving, forgiving, illuminating, healing, and redeeming Messiah.

In the stories in this passage, we witness two beautiful encounters filled with divine joy and prophetic revelation. Mary visits her cousin Elizabeth, who, despite her old age, is miraculously pregnant with John the Baptist. When Mary greets Elizabeth, the baby leaps in Elizabeth's womb, and she is filled with the Holy Spirit. Elizabeth exclaims, "Blessed are you among women, and blessed is the child you will bear!" (Luke 1:42). This moment is a profound recognition of God's work in their lives, prompting Mary to respond with her song of praise, the Magnificat.

Mary's Magnificat, a hymn of humble gratitude and profound trust in God's promises, is a revolutionary cry. It's not the timid voice of a teenage girl but the bold proclamation of a rebel, a radical, a prophet, a woman heralding the overturning of unjust and abusive leaders and systems. It foretells the toppling of exploitative economic, social, and

6

political structures, as the reign of God in Christ brings justice to the exploited, freedom to the oppressed, dignity to the despised, and the good things of God to those who have nothing. It's a revolutionary cry, as radical and pertinent today as it was two thousand years ago. Similarly, Zechariah's Benedictus echoes themes of deliverance, mercy, and the fulfillment of God's covenant.

May the words of Mary in Luke 1:46–55 transform our hearts, imaginations, and lives:

"My soul glorifies the Lord, and my spirit rejoices in God my Savior . . .

He has performed mighty deeds with his arm;
he has scattered those who are proud in their inmost thoughts.
He has brought down rulers from their thrones
but has lifted up the humble.
He has filled the hungry with good things
but has sent the rich away empty."

**Guiding Truth:** Mary and Zechariah's songs reveal God's revolutionary work of justice, mercy, and faithfulness, inviting us to embrace God's transforming presence.

**Reflection:** How can I embody the revolutionary spirit of Mary's Magnificat in addressing injustice and inequality in my community? How can I proclaim God's mercy and faithfulness, following Zechariah's example?

**Prayer:** Lord God, please fill our hearts with the joy and faith of Mary and Zechariah. Inspire us with Mary's prophetic, radical, revolutionary words. Please help us to recognize your presence in our lives and respond with songs of praise and trust. May your Spirit fill us and guide us in proclaiming your mercy and love. Teach us to see your hand in every moment and to surrender joyfully to your will. Amen.

# Day 3: Embracing God's Humble Arrival

## Reading: Luke 2:1–21

Jesus's birth is a mystery, as God became human and dwelt among us. In a simple stable surrounded by animals, the Savior of the world enters our human reality. Mary and Joseph, in their vulnerability and faith, welcome Jesus with open hearts, embodying a deep trust in God's plan.

The shepherds, marginalized and overlooked by society, are the first to receive the heavenly announcement. The angel proclaims, "Don't be afraid. I bring you good news that will cause great joy for all the people. Today in the town of David, a Savior has been born to you; he is the Messiah, the Lord" (Luke 2:10–11). Their response is immediate—they go to Bethlehem, where they find Mary, Joseph, and the baby lying in a manger. With hearts full of awe and wonder, they glorify and praise God, spreading the news of what they have witnessed. The heavenly hosts join the celebration of Jesus's birth, proclaiming, "Glory to God in the highest heaven, and on earth peace to those on whom his favor rests" (Luke 2:14). Heaven and earth join in proclaiming, welcoming, and celebrating the birth of Jesus Christ the Messiah.

Mary's courage and faith shine through this story. Young, vulnerable, and living under the shadow of empire, she stands with prophetic strength, bearing the weight of divine mystery in her body. She doesn't merely receive God's call—she sings of it, proclaims it, and surrenders to it with fierce trust. The incarnation isn't a sanitized event. It unfolds in the blood, sweat, and exhaustion of a young mother bringing the Son of the Living God into the world. The true scandal of the incarnation isn't in theological debates but in the raw, embodied reality of a girl carrying salvation in her womb, her placenta and body nurturing the Son of God, laboring in the dark, nursing the Christ with love and with tired and aching skin. Any telling of this story that ignores the weight she bore—both in her body and soul—misses the depth of the gospel itself. This is faith not in theory but in the flesh.

The birth of Jesus Christ calls us to embrace humility, openness, and readiness to witness God's transformative love and power. Mary's courage and prophetic insight remind us of the deep, often hidden, sacrifices involved in welcoming God's presence into our world and hearts.

**Guiding Truth:** The birth of Jesus invites us to embrace humility and trust, nurturing a readiness to welcome God's purpose and presence.

**Reflection:** How can I cultivate a heart of humility and openness like Mary? How can I respond to God's presence with awe and readiness, like the shepherds?

**Prayer:** Creator God, you reveal your love, humility, and power in Jesus's birth. Please help us to welcome you into our lives with the same trust and vulnerability as Mary and Joseph. May we, like the shepherds, respond to your presence with awe and joy, sharing your good news with others. Open our hearts to the scandal of the birth of Jesus Christ—God becoming human through the pain, vulgarity, and sacredness of childbirth. Teach us to embrace the hidden sacrifices and to recognize your transformative presence, love, and power in our everyday moments. Fill our hearts with the courage and prophetic insight to live faithfully in your light. Amen.

# Day 4: Dwelling in God's Presence

## Reading: Luke 2:22–52

The temple in Jerusalem buzzed with the ordinary practices of devotion when a young couple arrived, cradling their child. An older man, eyes clouded by years but heart sharp with expectation, took the infant in his arms and wept. "My eyes have seen your salvation." A prophet bent with time but aflame with holy fire confirmed the moment: redemption had drawn near.

Prophesying the arrival of the Messiah, Simeon exclaimed that Jesus is God's salvation, prepared by the Lord before all humanity and the nations, "a light for revelation to the Gentiles, and the glory of God's people Israel." The Messiah won't just reveal God's glory to the nations; he will "cause the falling and rise of many in Israel, be a sign spoken against, reveal the thoughts of many hearts, and act as a sword piercing the souls of generations" (Luke 2:28–32).

Later, in the same sacred space, the boy Jesus lingered long after his parents had left. When they found him, he spoke with clarity beyond his years: "Why were you searching for me? Didn't you know I had to be in my Father's house?" (Luke 2:49). For Jesus, lingering in the loving, holy presence of God filled him with peace and love, ignited his heart and imagination with divine fire, and clarified his purpose, identity, and destiny. There is no place like the presence of God for transforming our being, our hearts, our minds, our actions, our purpose, and our identity.

God's presence is warm, inviting, loving, and a refining, holy, and purifying furnace.

These moments in Luke's gospel unveil the collision of time and eternity. God is found in the waiting—Simeon, Anna, Mary, and Joseph, all moving in step with the slow unfolding of divine purpose. God is also found in the surprising, in the child who stays behind, who belongs to something greater than the expectations of family or culture.

This is where the passage unsettles us. We long for the certainty of a structured, predictable spirituality, yet God often moves outside our timelines, our safe assumptions, and our small certainties. Simeon and Anna teach us to wait with hope, even when the years are long, and silence weighs heavy. Jesus reminds us that true belonging is found in God's presence, even when that presence disrupts our familiar paths.

So, we ask: Where is God drawing near in the ordinary? Where is God unsettling our assumptions? Are we waiting well and willing to follow when God calls us beyond what we know?

How often do I resist the slow, sacred work of ordinary days? I crave the dramatic, the immediate, the unmistakable sign. But holiness unfolds in the unnoticed places—an old prophet's whispered prayer, a mother's quiet pondering, a child's curiosity. God's presence doesn't demand spectacle. It asks for attentiveness. God's presence primarily doesn't satisfy our longings and yearnings—it glorifies Jesus Christ.

**Guiding Truth:** Dwell in God's presence with open hands—ready to wait and be surprised.

**Reflection:** How is God inviting you to wait with trust rather than frustration? In what ways is God calling you beyond your familiar comforts into deeper belonging?

**Prayer:** God of the long waiting and the sudden revealing, open my eyes to see you in the ordinary. Teach me to wait with hope, to trust when I cannot see, and to follow even when it means leaving familiar things behind. Make my heart attentive to your presence, whether you come in whispers or the disruptive call of something new. May I, like Simeon and Anna, hold onto your promise, and máy I, like Jesus, find my true home in you. Amen.

# Day 5: A Baptism of Fire and Grace

**Reading: Luke 3**

John stands at the water's edge, calling, warning, pleading. "Repent, for the kingdom of God is near." He speaks with urgency, not to condemn but to awaken. The people come—soldiers, tax collectors, the weary, the desperate—each seeking renewal. But John refuses to offer them cheap reassurance. "Bear fruit in keeping with repentance." Transformation isn't a hollow ritual. It's a turning, a reorienting, a yielding to something deeper.

John is clear. He isn't the Messiah. Salvation isn't found in John. His role is to herald, announce, and make way for the Messiah. How often are we tempted to make the story about us, to enjoy the spotlight, and to think that we hold the answers, solutions, and personalities to make a difference? John knows better. "I baptize you with water. But one who is more powerful than I will come, the straps of whose sandals I am not worthy to untie. He will baptize you with the Holy Spirit and fire. His winnowing fork is in his hand to clear his threshing floor and to gather the wheat into his barn, but he will burn up the chaff with unquenchable fire" (Luke 3:16–17). John's entire life is dedicated to glorifying Jesus and proclaiming the good news of the Messiah (Luke 3:18). Would people say the same about my life and yours?

Then, Jesus steps into the water. The One without sin enters the baptism of repentance, standing in solidarity with those who are broken, lost, and longing. The heavens split. A voice declares love. The Spirit

13

descends like a dove. Here is the turning point—the moment when the Son is named, the kingdom is revealed, and the way of Jesus is set in motion.

This passage confronts us. It shakes us awake. It invites us beyond superficial faith into lives that reflect God's radical justice and mercy. Repentance isn't shame; it's freedom. It's an invitation to align our hearts with God's love, to abandon the illusions of self-sufficiency, and to step into a new way of being. A voice calls from heaven, "You are my Son, whom I love; with you, I am well pleased" (Luke 3:22). There can be no doubt. God has come in the flesh. Jesus is the Christ. We find salvation and restoration only in him.

God's salvation isn't merely personal renewal. It's the inbreaking of a kingdom where the lowly are lifted, the powerful are humbled, and love is the law. It calls us to integrity, generosity, and the hard work of reconciliation and justice. But we don't walk this road alone. Jesus has gone before us, stands with us, and empowers us.

**Guiding Truth:** Repentance isn't about guilt but an invitation into God's transforming love.

**Reflection:** What is God calling you to turn from, and what is God calling you toward? How does Jesus's baptism shape the way you live in the world?

**Prayer:** God of fire and mercy, strip away all that keeps me from you. Shape my heart in love, truth, and justice. Let my life bear fruit that reflects your grace. May my actions, heart, mind, and imagination glorify you, proclaim your shalom and gospel, and make way for your presence, glory, and salvation. May I decrease that Christ Jesus might increase. As Jesus stood in the waters, may I stand in your presence—renewed, forgiven, and ready to follow. Amen.

# Day 6: Strength in the Wilderness

## Reading: Luke 4:1–13

The Spirit leads Jesus into the wilderness, where hunger gnaws and silence stretches. For forty days, he's alone—except he isn't. The enemy is there, whispering, offering, twisting truth into something almost believable. "Turn these stones to bread." "Bow, and I'll give you power." "Prove who you are." Each temptation is a seduction of control, compromise, security, identity, self-sufficiency, and trust in God. Each is a lie.

When we're in the spiritual and personal wilderness, the world, flesh, and devil test our belief, faith, and trust in God. Henri Nouwen reminds us that the temptation to turn stones into bread is a test of our self-sufficiency and whether we will trust in God for provision, love, and care (Henri Nouwen, In the Name of Jesus). We naturally desire security and immediate gratification and often tend to define life in material terms by what we have and do and how others see us. But while we need food, shelter, clothing, and some material things, they can never wholly satisfy our spiritual needs. Only God's love and word can genuinely satisfy. Are you tempted to define yourself by what you have and do, by your material wealth and achievements? Or are you sustained by God's word and love?

The temptation to bow to power is about giving into moral and ethical compromise for control, power, influence, achievement, dominance, and security. But Jesus rejected earthly models of power and, instead, embraced the way of the cross and a life of humility, sacrificial

15

love, and service. Are you tempted to grasp power, control, and influence? Or are you surrendering to God's will and choosing the way of sacrificial love and service?

The temptation to jump from the temple is the temptation to test God and to reach for approval, validation, and external markers of identity. Instead, Jesus rejects this way and presses into the assurance of God's love, the desire to submit to God's goodness and will, and the affirmation that comes from God's approval, not the validation of people. Jesus knew God loved and held him—this didn't need testing. Are you testing God and divine assurance and defining yourself by what others think? Or are you resting in God's love for you that'll never waiver or change?

Jesus resists—not with displays of might, but with trust. He doesn't grasp power, demand comfort, or manipulate God. Instead, he leans into the unseen presence that sustains him. "It's written," he replies. He stands firm, not because he's untouched by struggle, but because his heart is anchored in truth.

This wilderness isn't just his. It's ours. We know the ache of hunger—not just for food, but for meaning, validation, and control. We hear the whispers that say we're what we have, what we do, what others think. We're tempted to grasp instead of trust, to dominate instead of serve, to demand rather than receive.

But Jesus shows another way—the way of surrender, the way of dependence, the way of trusting that God's presence, not worldly power, truly sustains. If we follow him, we'll face this wilderness, too. But we don't go alone. The same Spirit that led Jesus strengthens us, and the same love that sustained him holds us.

**Guiding Truth:** True strength isn't found in control but in trusting God's presence.

**Reflection:** What temptations in your life seek to replace trust with self-sufficiency? How is God inviting you to rely on love instead of power?

**Prayer:** God of the wilderness, when I'm tempted to grasp, teach me to trust. When I'm weak, remind me that your presence is enough. Form me in truth, sustain me in love, and lead me in the way of Jesus. Amen.

# Day 7: The Offense of Grace

## Reading: Luke 4:14–44

Jesus returns home, filled with Spirit-given power. In the synagogue, he reads from Isaiah: "The Spirit of the Lord is upon me . . . to bring good news to the poor, release to the captives, sight to the blind, freedom for the oppressed."

At first, the people marvel. They nod; they smile—until Jesus pushes further. He declares he's a prophet, in the tradition of Isaiah and Elijah, but also much more than that. Jesus claimed to be the fulfillment of Isaiah's prophecy and, therefore, the Messiah. Drawing upon two stories from the Hebrew Bible—Elijah and the Widow in Zarephath and Elisha and Naaman the Syrian—Jesus makes a scandalous, shocking, and, as far as many of his listeners are concerned, outrageous claims: God's healing, mercy, and salvation extend beyond Israel to the Gentiles—to outsiders, to those they considered unworthy. Jesus reminds them that God's mercy has always gone beyond the boundaries they expect. That grace reaches outsiders. That healing isn't for the privileged few.

Suddenly, admiration turns to fury. The crowd that welcomed him now drives him to the edge of a cliff. They expected the Messiah for Israel alone, who would restore Israel's power and prestige, elevate Israel, and overthrow Roman rule. But Jesus says he is the Messiah and that Messianic blessing and liberation would extend to outsiders, those despised, and even their oppressors. Jesus turned their expectations upside down, revealing God's grace as unpredictable, uncontrollable, extravagant, and for all. Instead of reinforcing religious, ethnic, and national pride, Jesus shows a kingdom that's about grace, not privilege— a grace that includes those we may despise.

This passage lays bare a deep human struggle: We love grace when it comforts us but resist it when it confronts us. We want a Savior who blesses us, not one who challenges our assumptions, shakes our complacency, and calls us beyond our safe circles. Jesus's listeners didn't want to be challenged. His words exposed their pride, self-righteousness, and hardness of heart. Do the words of Jesus pierce us the same way, exposing our pride and prejudice? Jesus called his listeners and you and me to radical humility, repentance, and inclusion. Jesus will not be confined to our limits. He moves outward—to the broken, the unclean, and the excluded. He heals, restores, casts out darkness, and will not be silenced.

So, we must ask: Where do we resist the unsettling reach of grace? Who have we deemed beyond the circle of God's love? Are we willing to follow Jesus where he goes—into the spaces of discomfort, reconciliation, and costly compassion?

The gospel is good news but not always comfortable news. It calls us to lay down our need for control and a false sense of entitlement and step into God's wild, boundary-breaking love.

**Guiding Truth:** God's grace is bigger than our boundaries—are we willing to embrace it?

**Reflection:** Where's Jesus inviting you to love beyond your comfort zone? How do you respond when grace challenges your expectations?

**Prayer:** Jesus, open my heart to the fullness of your grace. Break down my resistance, my fears, and my limits on love. Lead me beyond what feels safe and give me the courage to follow you into the places where mercy, justice, and healing are most needed. Amen.

# Day 8: Leaving Everything to Follow

Luke 5 is a chapter of holy disruption. Jesus steps into ordinary lives—fishermen at their nets, a leper in their suffering, a paralyzed person on their mat, a tax collector at their table—and calls them into something entirely new. This isn't just about individual transformation; it's about the in-breaking reign of God, overturning expectations, and redefining what it means to live faithfully.

When I'm most comfortable, the Spirit calls me to follow Jesus, disrupting my complacency, comfort, and ease. I may be in a professionally rewarding job, living in a city and house I'd never want to give up, or sitting in a church community I call home. None of those things are bad. But suddenly, the Spirit disrupts my comfort and calls me to follow Jesus where he leads. Discipleship is costly. God's call is surprising. And God's love and grace will carry us through the disruption, change, and costs that following Jesus often entails. But there isn't anything more fulfilling than letting go of our old and settled lives and following Jesus wherever he leads.

The miraculous catch of fish shows that Jesus provides more than we can imagine, but it's not the abundance of fish that matters—it's the willingness to leave it behind. Peter, James, and John walk away from their greatest professional success because they've encountered something greater. The healed leper and the paralyzed person find more than physical restoration; they find the freedom of forgiveness. Levi, the

21

tax collector, leaves wealth and security to host a banquet of grace, inviting outcasts to meet the One who calls sinners to repentance.

This chapter exposes the smallness of our trust and the bigness of Jesus's call. It challenges us to abandon comfort for discipleship, trade self-reliance for faith, and seek healing deeper than skin and success richer than wealth. This is the way of the gospel—a life of radical mercy, humility, and witness. It means leaving behind whatever binds us, whether fear, sin, pride, or complacency, and stepping into the abundant, risk-filled, joy-soaked life of following Jesus.

**Guiding Truth:** Jesus calls us to leave behind what holds us and step into the radical, transformative life of following and witnessing to God's kingdom.

**Reflection:** What is Jesus calling you to leave behind so you can follow more fully? How is your life bearing witness to the mercy and justice of God?

**Prayer:** Holy One, disrupt my comfort, shake my complacency, and draw me into deeper trust. Teach me to let go of what holds me back and step into the fullness of life in you. I struggle with fear and anxiety. I'm tempted by complacency and comfort. My heart often wants to go its own way and be the master of its own destiny. But I choose to follow you. I commit to leaving my old, comfortable, settled life behind. I'm entirely yours. You are my Lord and master, and where you lead me, I will follow. May my words and actions bear witness to your love and grace. Amen.

# Day 9: Restoring the Heart of the Law

## Reading: Luke 6:1–16

For most of my childhood and teens, I attended a Dutch Reformed School. I greatly value that upbringing, including the love for Scripture and the Creeds, the focus on liturgy and hymns, and the call to live a life that glorifies God and shares God's gospel and love in word and deed. But it could also be a legalistic setting at times, and I, like many of my peers, rebelled against those restrictions. Sometimes, the rules and regulations seemed at odds with the grace and freedom at the heart of the gospel. I don't want to overstate that because I'm so grateful for my childhood and the godly Dutch Reformed women and men who showed me Jesus's truth and love. But the temptation to forget the heart of the law and gospel is a real one that followers of Jesus face daily.

Luke 6:1–16 is a clash of visions. The religious leaders cling to a rigid, rule-bound faith, but Jesus unveils a kingdom where mercy, freedom, truth, justice, and healing reign. The Pharisees accuse Jesus's disciples of breaking Sabbath law by picking grain, yet Jesus reminds them that David himself took sacred bread when hungry. Then, in the synagogue, Jesus heals a person with a withered hand, exposing the Pharisees' hearts: they care more about rules than restoration.

This passage forces a reckoning. Do we see faith as a checklist or a living relationship? Do we use laws to control, or do we let God's mercy transform us? Jesus doesn't abolish the Sabbath—he restores its true meaning. The Sabbath was never meant to be a burden; it was always

23

about renewal, trusting God's provision, and stepping into the abundance of divine rest.

Then, Jesus does something striking—he calls twelve disciples. Jesus doesn't call the elite and powerful, but fishermen, a tax collector, and a zealot. This is the kingdom's heart: a people gathered not by status but by grace. Jesus calls the last and least, the respected and wealthy, the irresponsible and undisciplined, the unlikely and dismissed, the unruly and unrefined, the just and righteous, the outcast and broken, and everyone in between to follow him. The Spirit of Christ invites everyone to come to God, receive healing, restoration, and salvation, and follow Jesus wherever he leads. "The Spirit and the bride say, "Come!" And let the one who hears say, "Come!" Let the one who is thirsty come; and let the one who wishes take the free gift of the water of life" (Rev 22:17). Jesus invites us into a life where faith isn't about maintaining appearances but about radical love, healing, and calling others into the story of God.

**Guiding Truth:** Jesus invites us to move beyond lifeless religiosity into a living, breathing faith that heals, restores, and calls others into God's kingdom.

**Reflection:** Where is your faith bound by rules instead of being shaped by mercy and trust? How is Jesus calling you to bring healing and restoration into your community?

**Prayer:** God of mercy, break through my rigidness and fear. Teach me to live in the abundance of your grace. Shape my heart to love, heal, and call others into the beauty of your kingdom. Amen.

# Day 10: The Upside-Down Kingdom

**Reading: Luke 6:17–49**

In the international politics of recent years, we've been reminded, once again, of the seduction of power. Great nations—such as the United States, Russia, or China—use their wealth, militaries, cultural influence, and power to pressure, bully, coerce, and exploit smaller nations.

This dynamic isn't restricted to geopolitics, of course. During my years in church ministry and theological education, I've seen large churches and seminaries behave similarly, wielding their power for their benefit and growth, not necessarily to serve the least, last, struggling, and vulnerable, and often at the expense of ministries that are smaller than them. The world, flesh, and devil often tempt us to think and behave in ways that reflect our age's decaying, destructive spirits rather than the Spirit of Christ, the good news of the gospel, and the way of Jesus and his kingdom.

Luke 6:17–49 is a manifesto of God's kingdom—a world that runs against the grain of everything we assume about power, success, and righteousness. Jesus stands on a level place, surrounded by the desperate, sick, and outcast. He doesn't call them to self-improvement or religious performance. Instead, he blesses those experiencing poverty, hunger, sadness, and rejection. And Jesus warns the rich, satisfied, powerful, connected, respected, and praised. This isn't a sentimental spirituality; it's a radical reordering of reality.

Jesus calls for love that defies logic—love for enemies, generosity without expecting a return, and forgiveness that shatters cycles of retaliation. He asks, "Why do you call me 'Lord, Lord,' and don't do what I tell you?" Discipleship isn't admiration from a distance; it's obedience, trust, and transformation. It's building life on rock instead of sand.

The way of Jesus is costly. It demands surrender—of pride, grudges, and our obsession with security, power, control, and status. But it also brings freedom. Those who trust this upside-down kingdom find themselves unshaken, even when storms come because they stand not on self-sufficiency but on the unshakable foundation of God's mercy.

This passage pulls us into the heart of the gospel. Jesus's gospel isn't about external morality or theological correctness—it's about becoming the kind of person who reflects Christ, who embodies faith, hope, mercy, justice, righteousness, humility, and love. It's nothing less than a new way to be human.

**Guiding Truth:** Jesus calls us to build lives on the foundation of radical love, mercy, and obedience—an unshakable faith that transforms us and the world.

**Reflection:** Where do you resist the radical demands of Jesus's kingdom? How can you build your life on the foundation of love, forgiveness, and mercy?

**Prayer:** God of grace, reshape my heart. Teach me to love beyond what feels reasonable, to forgive as I have been forgiven, and to trust in your unshakable ways. Let my life be built on the foundation of your mercy and truth. Amen.

# Day 11: Faith that Amazes, Compassion that Restores

### Reading: Luke 7:1–17

Watching someone you love get taken by illness is its own kind of heartbreak. You're grieving before they're even gone. You see them slipping away bit by bit—sometimes in body, sometimes in mind—and you feel so helpless. You can't fix it. You can't stop it. All you can do is sit there, hold their hand, and try to love them through it. And then there's the pain when they die. I've had a few moments in life when I've lost people I love dearly. A couple of friends and family members have committed suicide, one dear friend died of cancer, and others died in their youth. The pain of losing someone you love stays with you for life. Your love for them rarely fades. You miss them so much, and all kinds of things bring back memories of them—a conversation, song, smell, date, scene, or photo.

Jesus understood this grief and loss and responded compassionately to those who suffered. Luke 7:1–17 has two such stories. One story is of a Roman centurion who's watching his beloved servant suffer and come close to death. The other story is of a woman who's just lost her son.

Luke 7:1–17 contains two encounters, each trembling with human vulnerability and divine mercy. First, a Roman centurion—an outsider and a man of authority—sends word to Jesus, not demanding but humbly trusting that a word alone will heal his servant. This is faith stripped of ego, faith that doesn't cling to entitlement or proximity but rests on the sheer confidence that Jesus has the authority to make things whole. Jesus is amazed.

Then, as Jesus approaches the village of Nain, another scene unfolds: a grieving widow burying her only child. There are no requests, no expressions of faith, only raw sorrow. But Jesus sees her. His heart breaks open with compassion, and without being asked, he interrupts the funeral procession with life. The dead man rises. The mother is restored. Hope breathes again.

Together, these stories pull us into a deeper truth. Faith isn't performance. It's surrender—letting go of control and trusting the One whose word holds life. Even when our faith feels absent or crushed under grief too heavy for words, Jesus moves toward us with tenderness. Healing doesn't always come as we expect, but mercy arrives anyway, breaking through the noise, silencing the funeral dirge, and lifting us up.

This is the shape of the kingdom of God: humility that amazes heaven, compassion that interrupts despair, and a Savior whose authority is matched only by boundless love. We follow this Jesus—a healer, restorer, and friend of the broken.

**Guiding Truth:** Jesus meets us in humble faith and unspeakable sorrow, bringing restoration where we thought there was only loss.

**Reflection:** Where's Jesus inviting you to trust with open hands? How might you embody compassion for those caught in grief and despair?

**Prayer:** God of mercy, meet me in my need—whether in faith or silence. Teach me to trust your healing word and embody your compassion to others. Let my life bear witness to your kindness and restoring power. Amen.

# Day 12: Grace for the Doubter and the Desperate

### Reading: Luke 7:18–50

Most of us go through periods in life where we feel doubt, desperation, or both. After years of Christian ministry and countless disappointments and hurts, I spent some of my thirties struggling to continue this Christian journey. Did I really believe anymore? Did I want to dedicate the rest of my life to Jesus and keep experiencing these hurts at the hands of his people? Was there a different and better way of life and belief system that I should choose? Those doubts were often interwoven with my desperation. I longed for rest, healing, friendship, and safety. If you've been through spiritual abuse or religious trauma, you know how desperation and doubt can often walk side by side.

Luke 7:18–50 is a collision of doubt, scandal, and extravagant grace. John the Baptist, imprisoned and disillusioned, sends messengers to ask the question many of us ask in our own dark nights: "Are you the One, or should we expect another?" Jesus doesn't scold the question. Instead, he points to the evidence of grace breaking loose—the blind see, the lame walk, the dead are raised, and the good news is preached to those experiencing poverty. Sometimes, when faith frays, we must be reminded that the kingdom of God is already stirring in places we thought were lifeless.

Then comes the scene in the Pharisee's house. An unnamed woman—sin clinging to her reputation like a shadow—bursts in, weeping. She anoints Jesus's feet with perfume and tears, wiping them with her hair. It's messy. It's inappropriate. It's scandalous. It's precious. It's beautiful. And it's offensive to those who believe holiness should keep its distance from sinners. But Jesus flips the script. He doesn't see her scandal but her love. While the religious elite recoil, Jesus welcomes her as the picture of forgiven devotion.

These two stories bind together. There's room in this kingdom for the doubter and the desperate. The Spirit of Christ invites and welcomes the one questioning if Jesus is real and the one so certain of his mercy they weep at his feet. What holds them both? Grace. Who embraces the doubter and the desperate? Christ Jesus. What sends us out from this story? Gratitude.

We follow a Jesus who honors honest doubt, welcomes scandalous love, and forgives sins that everyone else remembers.

**Guiding Truth:** Jesus meets our deepest doubts and worst failures with the relentless grace that sets us free.

**Reflection:** Where are you longing for Jesus to answer your questions or calm your doubts? How does love for Jesus show up in your daily actions and relationships?

**Prayer:** Merciful One, hold my questions, heal my shame, and fill me with the kind of love that spills over in worship. Teach me to see others through your eyes and to rest in the grace that never lets me go. Amen.

# Day 13: Hearing and Holding the Word

## Reading: Luke 8:1–21

Luke 8:1–21 calls us to listen—not just with ears, but with hearts ready to be transformed. Jesus moves through towns, preaching the good news, and alongside him are the twelve disciples and several women who have been healed and restored. Jesus challenges traditional power structures and clarifies that the gospel is for everyone regardless of social status, gender, culture, financial situation, or past failures. From the start, the passage upends assumptions—this kingdom isn't just for the elite or the powerful but for those willing to follow, including women once bound by shame and affliction.

God's kingdom is radically inclusive. In an age shaped by polarizations, divisions, and conflicts, we can easily exclude those who aren't like us. We can make them our enemies, refusing to see any good in them, their desire for a better world, or humanity. But Jesus calls us to a countercultural lifestyle of loving, honoring, and embracing others, including those we've traditionally rejected, despised, or excluded.

Then comes the parable of the Sower. Seeds scatter on different soils—some devoured by birds, some withering on rocky ground, some choked by thorns, and some sinking deep and bearing fruit. This is the story of every human heart. Some hear but never receive. Some embrace faith with enthusiasm but fall away when trouble comes. Others let the noise of wealth, worry, and comfort strangle their devotion. But then some listen, hold fast, and bear fruit with perseverance. It's too easy to hear God's Word and keep it at arm's length, preventing it from shaping our values, lifestyles, worldviews, and hearts. But those whose hearts are "good soil" listen to the Word, put it into action, allow it to transform their lives, and bear fruit in obedience, love, and perseverance.

Jesus moves to the parable of a lamp on a stand, proclaiming that our faith must be bright, noticeable, and illuminating, not hidden. Those who follow Jesus shine with the same love, justice, righteousness, and compassion as him. We do this through the way we talk, the decisions we make, the actions we choose, the priorities we set, the people we embrace, and through our suffering, service, and sacrifice.

Jesus ends with a striking statement: "My mother and brothers are those who hear God's word and put it into practice." Faith isn't about proximity to Jesus—it's about obedience. The real family of God is made up of those who receive the Word, let it take root, and live it out. We may love and honor our biological relatives, but spiritual kinship arises from faith and obedience, not blood or family ties.

So, the question isn't whether we hear Jesus but whether we let his words transform us. Will we be soil that bears fruit? Will we cultivate a faith that perseveres, resists distraction, and flourishes in love, justice, and witness?

**Guiding Truth:** True disciples don't just hear Jesus—they hold onto his Word and let it shape their lives.

**Reflection:** What distractions or struggles threaten to choke out your faith? How can you cultivate a heart that listens deeply and bears fruit in action?

**Prayer:** God of truth, soften my heart. Let your Word sink deep, take root, and bear fruit in my life. Free me from distractions and fears that keep me from following you fully. Help me hear, trust, and live in your way. Amen.

# Day 14: Faith in the Storm, Healing in the Touch

## Reading: Luke 8:22–56

Luke 8:22–56 tells three stories, but they are really one story: faith meeting the power of Jesus. The followers of Jesus see him bringing peace, liberation, resurrection, and healing wherever he goes. Yet, like us today, they must choose to have faith in the goodness, presence, love, and power of Jesus.

First, the disciples are caught in a furious storm. The boat is sinking, and Jesus is asleep. When they wake him, terrified, he rebukes the storm and their fear. The lesson? Faith trusts that Jesus is in control even when everything feels out of control. Jesus isn't just the Lord of all creation; he's the One who's present in our chaos, fears, anxieties, and pain, bringing peace and calm.

Then, Jesus meets a man possessed by demons, living among the tombs, isolated and tormented. With a word, Jesus drives out the legion of demons, restoring the man to wholeness. But instead of rejoicing, the townspeople beg Jesus to leave. They preferred their comfort over transformation. The healed man wants to follow Jesus, but Jesus sends him home instead to be a living testimony of mercy. Jesus restores us to right relationship with God, ourselves, and others, then gives us the joy of testifying to God's healing and salvation.

Finally, Jesus is interrupted on his way to heal a dying girl. A woman, bleeding for twelve years, reaches for the hem of his garment. Power goes out from him, and she is healed. Jesus stops, looks her in the eye, and calls her "daughter." Meanwhile, the delay seems fatal—Jairus's daughter dies. But Jesus enters the house, takes her by the hand, and raises her to life. What compassion our Savior has! What love for us and presence in our lives! Jesus calls us to trust in his power of sickness, sin, and death and his loving, merciful presence in our lives.

These stories teach us that faith isn't about controlling outcomes but trusting in Jesus, whether in storms, suffering, sickness, heartbreak, or even death itself. Jesus is never overwhelmed, never late, never uncompassionate, never unjust, never indifferent. He meets our fear with peace, our isolation with love, and our death with life.

**Guiding Truth:** Jesus calls us to trust him fully, knowing he has power over every storm, every wound, and even death.

**Reflection:** Where in your life do you need to trust Jesus more deeply? How is Jesus calling you to share his mercy with others?

**Prayer:** Jesus, in my storms, in my suffering, in my fears, help me trust you. Heal what is broken in me, calm what is anxious, and lead me into deeper faith. May my life bear witness to your power and love. Amen.

# Day 15: Give Them Something to Eat

Luke 9:1–17 begins with Jesus sending out the twelve. He gives them power and authority but tells them to take nothing for the journey: no staff, no bread, no money, no extra tunic. Why? Because the mission isn't fueled by self-sufficiency but by trust. The kingdom of God advances through weakness, dependence, service, and hospitality.

As disciples, one of the hardest lessons in life is trusting God. Jesus has given us power, protection, presence, and provision, but we still find it hard to depend on God. Yet, we can do nothing in our strength. We must go wherever Jesus sends us, proclaim his good news, share his love, live in his righteousness, and offer his healing—and we can only do these things with his empowering presence.

Then Herod appears, confused and disturbed by the movement spreading in Jesus's name. Power is always unsettled by grace it can't control. Jesus, unfazed, gathers his disciples for rest, but the crowds follow. And rather than turning them away, Jesus welcomes them, teaches them, heals them.

As the day fades, the disciples see scarcity: "Send the crowd away." But Jesus responds, "You give them something to eat." They have five loaves and two fish—a lunchbox in the face of a multitude. Yet Jesus takes, blesses, breaks, and gives it. And somehow, everyone is fed. There's even more left over than they started with.

This passage moves from mission to scarcity to miracle. And at the center is Jesus, the One who calls us to trust, serve, and offer what little we have. He invites us to step into impossible situations with open hands, not because we have enough, but because he is enough. God doesn't just provide for those of us who are disciples; God showers blessings, provisions, and care on all humanity and creation. God is more generous, loving, just, holy, and faithful than we could ever hope, dream, or imagine. In this passage, the disciples are reminded of this repeatedly as they learn to trust in God's provision, revealed in Jesus Christ.

In a world of exhaustion, hunger, and fear, this story reminds us that we aren't spectators but participants in the miracle.

**Guiding Truth:** Jesus invites us to trust him with our insufficiency and join him in feeding the world with grace, truth, and compassion.

**Reflection:** Where do you feel most inadequate in your calling or service? What might Jesus ask you to offer, even if it feels small?

**Prayer:** Jesus, take what little I have, including my gifts, my time, and my trust, and multiply it for your kingdom. Teach me not to see what I lack but what you can do when I give myself to you. I am weak; you are strong. I have nothing; you have everything. I don't know what to do; you have sovereign plans and purposes. I lack courage; you give boldness. I'm wounded and broken; you offer healing. Teach me to trust and rely on your love, compassion, and goodness. Amen.

# Day 16: The Way of the Cross

## Reading: Luke 9:18–62

Luke 9:18–62 is a turning point. Jesus asks his disciples, "Who do you say I am?" and Peter replies, "The Christ of God." But Jesus doesn't follow this with talk of victory or thrones. Instead, he speaks of rejection, suffering, death, and resurrection. The Messiah will not conquer by force but by laying down his life.

Then comes the more challenging part: "If anyone would come after me, let them deny themselves, take up their cross daily, and follow me." The way of Jesus isn't self-promotion but self-surrender. It's not about finding life through control, power, or achievement but by losing it, giving it away in love, and trusting that what feels like loss is the path to resurrection.

On the mountaintop, Jesus is transfigured—radiant, glorious, unmistakably divine. Yet even here, the voice from the cloud doesn't say, "Be amazed," but "Listen to him." Glory isn't revealed in spectacle but in obedience.

The rest of the chapter presses this point. The disciples argue about who's greatest. They try to shut down someone casting out demons because he's not part of their group. They want to call down fire on a Samaritan village. Repeatedly, they miss the heart of the gospel.

Jesus isn't just teaching us about humility, mercy, and mission; he's living it. He sets his face toward Jerusalem. He knows what lies ahead.

The call to follow him is real and costly. Excuses won't do. Comfort, family, and even good things must take second place to the reign of God.

This passage reminds us that following Jesus isn't a sentimental journey. It's a radical reordering of our lives around the cruciform love of Christ. And yet, paradoxically, it's the path to true life, joy, and peace.

**Guiding Truth:** To follow Jesus means surrendering everything daily and discovering life on the other side of the cross.

**Reflection:** What am I holding onto that keeps me from fully following Jesus? In what ways is Jesus inviting me to take up my cross today?

**Prayer:** Jesus, teach me to follow you, not with conditions but with courage. Help me release control, ego, and fear. Let your cross shape my life, and may I trust you as I walk in your footsteps daily. Amen.

# Day 17: Sent with Joy, Rooted in Grace

## Reading: Luke 10:1–24

I remember one of the first times I was trusted with a ministry. I was in my late teens, and a pastor allowed me to preach. The night before the sermon, I felt physically sick. My heart was overwhelmed by a mix of excitement, insecurity, anxiety, hope, and fear. Would I be up to the task my pastor had entrusted to me?

Luke 10:1–24 is a breathtaking picture of mission, vulnerability, and joy. Jesus sends out seventy-two followers in pairs, like seeds scattered into villages and towns. He doesn't offer them security or prestige. Instead, he sends them with urgency and dependence—no money, no bag, no backup plan—just peace, presence, and the gospel.

They're told to enter homes humbly, receive hospitality without demanding more, and proclaim the nearness of God's reign. Whether welcomed or rejected, they must bear witness to something greater than themselves. This isn't coercive evangelism; it's a way of living that embodies peace, trust, healing, and hope.

When the seventy-two return, they're bursting with excitement: "Even the demons submit to us!" But Jesus redirects their joy. Don't rejoice in power or visible success, he says. "Rejoice that your names are written in heaven." Our worth doesn't rest in results but in relationships. Our belonging in God's kingdom is the deepest joy of all.

Jesus then prays with deep emotion, praising God for hiding these things from the wise and revealing them to the childlike. This kingdom doesn't belong to the clever or accomplished; it belongs to the humble, the open, and the receptive. He turns to the disciples and says, "Blessed are the eyes that see what you see."

This passage reminds us we are sent ones. We don't have pressure to control outcomes; we have the freedom to trust, serve, and witness. And we are held, not by what we do for Jesus, but by what he has done for us.

The call is clear: live sent, walk humbly, rejoice deeply—not in success, but in the grace that carries your name.

**Guiding Truth:** Jesus sends us into the world with peace, humility, and joy rooted not in success but in our identity as beloved children of God.

**Reflection:** Where are you being sent to bring peace, healing, or hope? Is your joy grounded in what you do for Jesus or in who you are in him?

**Prayer:** Jesus, send me where you will. Let me carry peace, receive humbly, speak hope, and rejoice not in success but in being yours. Let my joy be rooted in grace and my life a witness to your love. Amen.

# Day 18: The Disruptive Way of Love

## Reading: Luke 10:25–42

Luke 10:25–42 holds two well-known stories that, side by side, reveal something radical about love and discipleship. A legal expert asks Jesus a loaded question: "What must I do to inherit eternal life?" Jesus turns it back to him, leading to the great commandments: love God and neighbor. But the man wants to narrow the definition: "Who's my neighbor?" In response, Jesus tells the parable of the Good Samaritan.

A man is beaten and left for dead. A priest and a Levite pass by. These men are religious leaders, perhaps too concerned with purity, fear, or simply staying on schedule. But a Samaritan stops. He's an outsider and despised. He sees the wounded man, is moved by compassion, and acts with generosity and courage. He binds wounds, lifts the man onto his animal, pays for his care, and promises more.

Jesus's point is jarring: the neighbor isn't someone you choose to love but someone who shows love, even when it costs. The one who acts with mercy is the one who fulfills the law. Love, then, isn't defined by boundaries but by action.

Many forces in society encourage us to be hard-hearted or judgmental toward those who differ from us. We're encouraged to fear, exclude, judge, dismiss, and wish for the worst. Yet Jesus modeled the opposite—loving, honoring, including, protecting, and valuing those who differ from us and who often reveal God to us.

Then we move from the road to a home. Martha is busy with good things, such as serving, preparing, and hosting. Mary sits at Jesus's feet, listening. Martha grows frustrated, and Jesus responds tenderly: "You're worried and distracted by many things, but only one thing is necessary."

Presence and attentiveness are sacred forms of worship and surrender to God. Unless we slow down and seek stillness, silence, and attention, we'll find it challenging to have intimacy with Jesus or become like him.

Together, these stories challenge two distortions: a life of faith that avoids costly compassion and one that's so distracted by good work that it forgets the better way of presence. Jesus invites us into deep love for our neighbors and undistracted intimacy with him. Action without presence burns out, and presence without compassion becomes empty.

**Guiding Truth:** Love that transforms the world flows from a heart rooted in Jesus's presence and compassion.

**Reflection:** Who's Jesus calling you to love with sacrificial, boundary-breaking mercy? What distractions might be keeping you from sitting at Jesus's feet?

**Prayer:** Jesus, open my heart to love without limits and to listen without hurry. Shape me into someone who chooses compassion on the road and communion in the secret place. Let my hands, mind, and heart be yours. Amen.

# Day 19: Learning to Pray Like Jesus

**Reading: Luke 11:1–13**

In Luke 11:1–13, Jesus doesn't just pray; he teaches others how to pray. Watching Jesus's intimacy with God, one disciple dares to ask: "Lord, teach us to pray." It's not a request for words or ritual. It's a longing to be drawn into the same deep well of connection that Jesus seems to live from.

Prayer doesn't begin with technique but with a hunger to share in Jesus's spirituality and intimacy with God. The desire to pray well is a work of grace, a gift from the Spirit, pulling us into deeper communion with the Divine.

Jesus responds with what's now called the Lord's Prayer. But it's more than a formula. It's a vision. Jesus offers a way of praying that orients us around trust, surrender, and simplicity. It begins with intimacy—"Father"—and reverence—"Hallowed be your name." Then come requests for daily sustenance, forgiveness, and protection. This isn't performative or lofty. It's grounded in the raw needs and desires of everyday life. True prayer holds together awe and dependence, worship and desire, intimacy and reverence. We name God holy while asking for bread, an approach to prayer that grounds us in daily trust and open-hearted surrender.

Jesus follows the prayer with two stories: a friend at midnight and a parent giving gifts. In both, the point isn't that God is reluctant but more generous than we dare believe. We're encouraged to ask, seek, and knock, not because we must pry open heaven's gates but because God longs to give.

The promise? "How much more will your heavenly Father give the Holy Spirit to those who ask." This is the heart of it all. Prayer isn't just about getting things; it's about receiving God's presence. The Spirit is the gift beyond all gifts: the power, comfort, wisdom, and the life of Christ within us.

God's love and presence are the most profound answer to every prayer. As God draws near, the Spirit comforts, challenges, and reshapes us from within. The Spirit isn't an accessory to prayer but our enabler, comforter, and fulfillment—God's gift that makes all other gifts possible.

This passage teaches us that prayer isn't about mastering a technique or persuading a reluctant deity. It's about becoming the kind of person who trusts God enough to ask, leans into relationships, and believes that even in silence or delay, something holy is happening.

**Guiding Truth:** Prayer is the bold, daily act of trusting in God's goodness and opening our lives to the transforming gift of the Spirit.

**Reflection:** What keeps you from asking, seeking, or knocking in prayer? How might your prayers shift if you fully trusted God's desire to give the Spirit?

**Prayer:** God, teach me to pray, not just with words but with trust. I need to surrender to your timing, sovereignty, and mystery. Please help me ask boldly, wait patiently, and open my heart fully to your Spirit. Even when my prayers feel delayed, please draw me closer to Jesus's heart and keep me attuned to your divine love and grace. Let prayer become not a task but a way of living in your presence. Amen.

# Day 20: Woe and Wonder

## Reading: Luke 11:14–54

Jesus constantly overturns the expectations and demands of religious leaders and his followers. His compassion, justice, righteousness, and interpretations of the Hebrew Bible confront their prejudices, religiosity, and sin. He's the Messiah, untamed by the norms and expectations of humanity. Each action and teaching reveals God in all God's fullness.

A demon is cast out, and instead of awe, there's an accusation. Jesus drives out demons by the power of demons, they say. The crowd, conditioned by suspicion, can't receive a miracle unless it fits their categories. Others demand a sign as if the healing wasn't one and the liberation of a bound soul wasn't enough to disturb their certainties.

Jesus, unshaken, speaks of divided kingdoms and restless spirits, but he's not just talking about exorcisms. He's unveiling the fractured inner life of a generation addicted to appearances and resistant to transformation. He calls them to wholeness, integrity, and a house swept and filled, not just emptied. Jesus challenges them to seek a light that isn't hidden and wisdom that doesn't perform.

When a woman blesses Jesus with words of affirmation, he redirects the moment: Blessed are those who hear and keep the word of God. This isn't piety for the sake of status. Jesus calls his listeners to obedience that births freedom, listening that leads to justice, and holiness that humbles.

46

Then, the tone shifts. Jesus denounces the religious elite. Not because they lead but because they lead with masks. They tithe but neglect love. They honor prophets who are long dead but silence the living ones. They burden others with legalism while refusing to be touched by the cost of grace.

This isn't a gentle correction. These are prophetic wounds offered to people who prefer polished externals to inner truth. And still, Jesus speaks. Still, he exposes, not to shame, but to invite. To illuminate. To save.

This text confronts our divided hearts in a world saturated with spiritual performance and cultural hypocrisy. It invites us to let the light in and stop polishing the outside of the cup while the inside rots. Jesus doesn't seek admiration. Jesus seeks honesty. Surrender. Wholeheartedness.

**Guiding Truth:** Jesus calls us out of spiritual performance and into radical honesty so that healing and light can enter every corner of our lives.

**Reflection:** Where in my life am I more invested in appearances than in inner transformation? How might I allow the light of Jesus to expose and heal what I'd rather keep hidden?

**Prayer:** Loving Truth, shine into the hidden places of my heart. Strip away my masks. Teach me to live from a place of integrity, love, and grace. Let my life reflect not religion but the beauty of your transforming presence. Amen.

# Day 21: Living Unveiled

## Reading: Luke 12

Luke 12 isn't a gentle stroll through spiritual sentiment; it's a summons. Jesus, surrounded by a pressing crowd, speaks not to the masses but to the disciples. The words are raw and urgent, pulling the veil off the soul of a culture obsessed with masks, wealth, control, and fear.

It begins with hypocrisy: the kind of hypocrisy that festers in religious performance and social self-preservation. Jesus warns what's hidden will be revealed; what's whispered in the dark will be shouted from the rooftops. These words cut deep into a world where image is everything and truth is commodified. The invitation is clear: live unveiled. Let honesty mark your life, not for exposure's sake, but for liberation.

Jesus moves from masks to fear. Don't fear those who can kill the body. Fear the One who holds the soul. And yet this holy fear is wrapped in staggering tenderness. Sparrows aren't forgotten. You're worth more than many sparrows. This isn't fear to terrify but to realign: a fear that anchors us in God's vast love and fierce holiness.

Then Jesus speaks of greed. A man asks for justice over inheritance, and Jesus answers with a parable of a rich fool: building barns, stockpiling security, and dying empty. Life doesn't consist in abundance. The kingdom isn't built on consumption. Instead, store treasures in heaven. Be rich toward God. Live ready, like servants with lamps lit, alert to the movements of grace.

48

And then: fire. Division. Urgency. Jesus hasn't come to affirm cultural niceties or religious comfort zones. The gospel disrupts. It sets households and systems trembling. The question isn't whether conflict will come but whether we can read the signs and be awake to the hour.

This is Jesus unfiltered. This isn't a tame spirituality. It's a call to discipleship with spine and soul.

**Guiding Truth:** Jesus calls us to live with courageous honesty, radical trust, and urgent faithfulness in a world built on fear, denial, and illusion.

**Reflection:** What masks am I still wearing to appear righteous or secure? How might I live more awake to the presence and purposes of Jesus today?

**Prayer:** Jesus, please strip me of illusion. Awaken me to the truth, even when it burns. Teach me to live with open hands, clear eyes, and a soul lit by your fire. Let my life bear the weight and beauty of your kingdom. Amen.

# Day 22: The Urgency of Mercy

**Reading: Luke 13:1–17**

In Luke 13:1–17, Jesus confronts a familiar lie: that tragedy always means guilt, suffering is punishment, and calamity must be earned. A tower falls. Blood is spilled. The crowd wants a moral scapegoat, but Jesus refuses to feed their appetite for blame. He asks, "Do you think they were more guilty than all the others living in Jerusalem? 5 I tell you, no! But unless you repent, you too will all perish" (Luke 13:4b–5).

This isn't a divine threat but divine clarity. Repentance isn't groveling. It's a return to truth and a turning toward life. Repentance is a refusal to live asleep while the kingdom stands at the door. Jesus then tells a story of a fruitless fig tree. It has taken up space for years, absorbed light, and given nothing back. The owner says, "Cut it down! Why should it use up the soil?" (Luke 13:7b). But the gardener, who's gentle, patient, and urgent, pleads for one more year. One more chance. One more breath of grace.

And then comes a living parable. A woman bent over for eighteen years, folded by suffering and made small by affliction. On the Sabbath, in the synagogue, Jesus sees her. He doesn't wait for permission. He calls her forward, speaks freedom, lays healing hands on her, and she straightens. She praises. She becomes whole in full view of the religious establishment, and they're indignant.

Jesus calls them out. You untie animals on the Sabbath, but not daughters of Abraham? Hypocrisy always makes peace with systems that

50

dehumanize while defending structures that maintain appearances. But Jesus breaks the silence. Jesus defies the order. Jesus heals on holy ground and reveals that compassion is never off duty.

This passage summons us to repent not only of personal sin but also of collective apathy. It's a call to bear fruit that feeds the hungry, refuses false narratives about the suffering, and joins Jesus in bending toward the broken with urgency, tenderness, and holy defiance.

**Guiding Truth:** Jesus invites us to lead lives of repentance, mercy, and justice, bearing fruit and breaking chains in a world that too often clings to blame and control.

**Reflection:** Where have I embraced judgment when Jesus invites compassion? What parts of my life remain fruitless, waiting for the mercy of repentance and renewal?

**Prayer:** Gardener of grace, loosen what binds me. Teach me to repent, not in shame, but in hope. Make me one who bears fruit, heals wounds, and lives with holy urgency. Amen.

# Day 23: The Narrow Door and the Wide Mercy

## Reading: Luke 13:18–35

The kingdom of God begins small. A mustard seed in the soil. Yeast hidden in dough. In a world captivated by power, speed, and spectacle, Jesus dares to name the unnoticed—the gentle work of transformation that begins in secret and ends in abundance. What God is building doesn't arrive by force. It grows slowly, steadily, almost invisibly, until it reorders everything.

Then the tone shifts. "Make every effort to enter through the narrow door." This isn't a call to exclusivity, but to urgency and depth. The narrow door isn't small because God is stingy: it's narrow because it can't be entered with baggage. Ego won't fit. Entitlement won't squeeze through. Neither will spiritual complacency or the illusion of control. This is the door of surrender.

Jesus warns that some will assume familiarity is enough. They'll say, "We ate with you. We heard you teach." But to hear isn't to follow. To be near isn't to be known. Discipleship isn't about proximity but transformation. It's not enough to sit at the table, we must be changed by the Host.

And yet, even here, grace breaks in. "People will come from east and west, north and south." The door may be narrow, but the invitation is wide. The last will be first. The outsider brought in. Those long dismissed will be seated in the kingdom's joy.

Jesus ends with lament. He aches over Jerusalem, the city that kills the prophets. He longs to gather its people like a hen gathers chicks under wings of safety, but they resist. Still, Jesus presses on, undeterred by threats or hardness of heart, walking the path of costly love. This is the Jesus we follow: the One who grieves, invites, warns, and loves to the end.

**Guiding Truth:** The kingdom of God grows in hidden ways, demands wholehearted surrender, and welcomes all who yield to the love and call of Jesus.

**Reflection:** What am I trying to carry through the narrow door that needs to be laid down? Where might I be resisting the slow, hidden work of the kingdom of God in my life or community?

**Prayer:** Jesus, give me the courage to surrender, the faith to walk the narrow path, and the vision to see the kingdom growing in small, unlikely places. Gather me in your mercy and make me new. Teach me to trust the slow work of grace, to welcome the outsider, to release what hinders love, and to follow you with humility and joy. Amen.

# Day 24: The Table of the Humble

## Reading: Luke 14:1–14

Jesus is invited to dine at the house of a prominent Pharisee, but this is no simple meal. It's a setup. The air is thick with judgment, posturing, and silence. A man suffering from swelling stands before him: uninvited, unseen by the powerful, yet fully seen by Jesus. And this happens on the Sabbath, which gives the story extra potency. Jesus asks: Is it lawful to heal on the Sabbath or not? They say nothing. So, Christ heals the man and sends him on his way. Mercy doesn't wait for permission.

Then Jesus turns to the table, and the places of honor being claimed like prizes. He tells a story, not just of etiquette, but of the kingdom of heaven. When you're invited, take the lowest place. Those who exalt themselves will be humbled, and those who humble themselves will be exalted. This isn't a clever way to get ahead. It's a radical reordering of power, status, and worth. Humility and service are at the heart of Jesus's message and example. The Way of Jesus is the path of sacrifice, humility, service, and love, and those who desire status and power won't be honored by Christ on the final day.

Finally, Jesus turns to his host and says what no one else dares to say: When you give a banquet, don't invite those who can pay you back. Invite those experiencing poverty, disability, and struggles; then you'll be blessed. True hospitality makes room for the ones society forgets. True kingdom living breaks cycles of reciprocity and replaces them with grace. Those who follow Jesus display generosity, inclusivity, and humility in ways that shock and scandalize religion and society but that give glory to God.

This passage confronts modern spiritual life, which is too often shaped by status, image, performance, productivity, and the subtle economics of influence. Jesus exposes our addiction to recognition and invites us to a deeper way: a table where the overlooked are honored, the hurting are healed, and pride has no seat.

Jesus is the Host of that table. He invites without agenda. He heals without hesitation. He humbles the proud and lifts up the lowly. Our tables are often too small and exclusive. But when we follow the way of the heavenly Host, we set a large, inclusive, generous table, which becomes home to the least and last, mirroring the example of Christ, and the hosts gathered on the final day to worship and glorify God.

**Guiding Truth:** Jesus calls us to reject status-seeking and embrace a life of humility, mercy, and radical hospitality that mirrors the kingdom of God.

**Reflection:** Where am I tempted to seek recognition rather than offer welcome? Who is missing from the table I've been given to set?

**Prayer:** Jesus, free me from the need to climb, compete, or impress. Teach me to sit low, serve quietly, and invite those who can't repay. Help me imitate your humility, follow your way of service and love, and include all those you call family. Let my life reflect the mercy and humility of your kingdom. Amen.

# Day 25: The Cost of the Invitation

**Reading: Luke 14:15–35**

One of the dinner guests hears Jesus speak about humility and hospitality and responds with a burst of religious optimism: "Blessed is the one who will eat at the feast in the kingdom of God!" It's the kind of thing people say when they want to sound holy but stay comfortable. Jesus doesn't rebuke him directly. Instead, he tells a story, a parable that pierces through the surface.

A great banquet is prepared, and the invitations are sent. The host longs to fill the table. But one by one, the guests offer excuses. A field, some oxen, a wedding: none of them evil, but all revealing a heart distracted by possession, progress, and personal comfort. The banquet is ready, but their hearts are full of something else.

So, the host sends the servant to the streets, the margins, and the broken. Those experiencing disabilities and poverty are welcomed with open arms. Still, there's room. The invitation expands to the highways and hedges, to the outsiders of outsiders. The table of the kingdom is shockingly open, but not everyone comes. Not because the door is shut but because their hearts are elsewhere.

Then Jesus turns to the crowd and speaks unsettled words: "Whoever doesn't hate father and mother, wife and children, cannot be my disciple." He's not preaching hatred; he's confronting idolatry. Anything we place above Christ, even good and beautiful things, becomes a barrier to the kingdom.

Discipleship isn't casual. It's costly. To follow Jesus is to carry a cross, to leave behind safety, approval, and even identity as the world defines it. It means counting the cost, relinquishing control, and surrendering comfort. The salt that loses its saltiness is useless, not because it vanishes but because it forgets what it's for.

This passage is a seismic jolt in a culture that worships convenience, speed, and self. The invitation is real. The feast is ready. But Jesus asks more than polite attendance: he asks for everything.

The One who tells this story also sets the table with his own body and blood. He invites and welcomes, but he doesn't water down the terms. Grace is free, but discipleship costs your life.

**Guiding Truth:** The kingdom of God is a lavish feast that is freely offered, but to enter it, we must leave behind everything that keeps us from wholehearted discipleship.

**Reflection:** What distractions or loyalties dull my response to Jesus's invitation? Am I counting the cost of discipleship or simply hoping to eat without change?

**Prayer:** Jesus, awaken me from comfort and distraction. Teach me to treasure your invitation above every possession, ambition, and relationship. Give me the courage to count the cost and grace to follow you wherever you lead. Let my life be salt, rich with flavor, purpose, and love. Shape me into one who lives fully for you. Amen.

# Day 26: The Joy of the Lost Found

**Reading: Luke 15**

Luke 15 opens with a scandal. The wrong people are drawing near. The tax collectors, sinners, disreputable, and undeserving crowd around Jesus, hungry not just for food but for grace. The religious elite murmur their disapproval: "This one welcomes sinners and eats with them." These religious leaders think grace should come with a gate, and love must be earned.

Jesus responds, not with rebuttal, but with three parables that build a symphony of mercy. A shepherd leaves ninety-nine sheep to seek one that's wandered. A woman lights a lamp and sweeps the house until her one lost coin is found. A father watches the horizon for a son who squandered everything.

The stories are simple, but their weight is anything but light. Each loss is costly. Each search is relentless. And each recovery ends not in a scolding but in celebration. Rejoice with me, they say. What was lost is found.

But the crescendo of this chapter isn't just in the younger son returning but in the older son refusing to join the party. This one stayed home, did everything right, and followed all the rules, but his heart grew cold. "I've worked for you," he says, "and you never threw a party for me." He cannot see that his bitterness has estranged him from his father just as much as his brother's rebellion.

This is where the parable meets the modern soul. In a society addicted to merit, image, and reward, we struggle with the kind of grace that throws parties for the undeserving. We're prone to comparison, exclusion, and hoarding forgiveness as if it were ours to dispense. But Jesus unmasks our resentment and calls us to join the feast of mercy.

Luke 15 teaches that God isn't stingy with grace. God seeks. God restores. God rejoices. Whether we've wandered far or simmered in silent pride, God invites us to come home and make space for others to come, too.

Jesus is the one telling these stories because Jesus is the one embodying them. He is the Good Shepherd who goes into the wilderness. The Woman who sweeps until the coin is found. The Father who runs and embraces. And the Host who pleads with the elder sibling to lay down anger and come inside.

**Guiding Truth:** The heart of God relentlessly seeks the lost and rejoices in their return, calling all to abandon pride and join the celebration of grace.

**Reflection:** In what ways have I distanced myself from God through rebellion or resentment? Who in my life is God calling me to welcome with joy, not judgment?

**Prayer:** God of mercy, meet me in my wandering and pride. Break open my heart with compassion. Teach me to celebrate redemption, not just for myself but for others. Please give me the courage to return when I'm far off and the humility to rejoice when others come home. Let my life echo your joy. Amen.

# Day 27: Faithful With Little, Faithful With Much

## Reading: Luke 16:1–18

Luke 16 opens with one of Jesus's most puzzling parables: the story of a dishonest manager. Facing termination, the manager slashes debts owed to his master, hoping to secure goodwill for his uncertain future. Strangely, the master commends the manager's shrewdness, not his dishonesty but his urgent, imaginative use of what he had, knowing his time was short.

Jesus isn't celebrating deceit. He is inviting us to see money and all worldly resources through the lens of eternity. He says, "Use worldly wealth to gain friends for yourselves so that when it's gone, you will be welcomed into eternal dwellings" (Luke 16:9). In other words, leverage the temporary for the eternal. Let your use of money reflect the values of the coming kingdom: generosity, justice, mercy.

Then Jesus utters something that should shake us: "You cannot serve both God and money" (Luke 16:13). These aren't two neutral forces. One will always pull you from the other. Our culture says wealth offers freedom, status, and control. But Jesus insists it's a rival god, demanding loyalty and shaping hearts. The one who is faithful in little will be faithful in much. We don't prove our faithfulness in abundance but in handling small, unseen, everyday choices.

When the religious elite sneer, Jesus exposes the root: "You justify yourselves before others, but God knows your hearts" (Luke 16:15). This warning still stands in a society obsessed with image and public virtue. What we treasure reveals who we serve, and what we justify often exposes what we fear losing.

Then, Jesus speaks about law, the enduring truth of God's ways, and the sanctity of covenant. "Anyone who divorces . . . and marries another commits adultery" (Luke 16:18). This verse is often wielded as a weapon rather than a window. But Jesus isn't offering legalism. He's confronting a culture where men discard women easily, often for personal gain or convenience. Divorce then was frequently an economic and social death sentence for women. Jesus is calling for the restoration of covenant faithfulness, not the condemnation of those who have sought remarriage through grief, abuse, or abandonment.

In a world fractured by relational pain, Jesus doesn't shame the broken; he upholds dignity, calls for responsibility, and protects the vulnerable. The grace of God doesn't vanish when vows are broken. Mercy still flows. Healing is still possible. Jesus is always on the side of restoration, never humiliation.

**Guiding Truth:** Jesus calls us to steward money, relationships, faith, and everything else with eternal urgency, fierce integrity, and grace-filled accountability.

**Reflection:** How does my use of money reflect what I truly value? Am I living with the kind of integrity and compassion Jesus calls "faithful"?

**Prayer:** Eternal God, teach me to be faithful with what you've placed in my hands. Help me resist the false security of wealth and the fear of losing status. Shape my heart to treasure what matters to you. Let integrity and mercy guide me in every relationship, transaction, and secret place. Amen.

# Day 28: The Great Reversal

**Reading: Luke 16:19–31**

This story contrasts the rich man and Lazarus, showing that if people don't listen to Moses and the Prophets, their hearts will be closed, and their ears and eyes will be shut even when astonishing miracles occur.

There was a rich man clothed in purple, feasting every day, and there was Lazarus, covered in sores, lying at the gate, longing for crumbs. One lived in comfort, the other in agony. But when death came, their positions reversed. The one who had everything ends up in torment. The one who had nothing is carried to rest in Abraham's arms.

This is no soft parable. It doesn't soothe. It confronts. It exposes the chasm between what the world celebrates and what eternity reveals. Not once in the story does the rich man acknowledge Lazarus by name while he lives. Even in the afterlife, he treats him like a servant. But heaven knows the name of those experiencing poverty. Heaven remembers the forgotten.

Jesus isn't saying wealth is evil. He's making it unmistakably clear: indifference is evil, sinful, and contradictory to the ways and revelations of God. The sin here isn't luxury; it's blindness. The gate wasn't far. The need wasn't hidden. The suffering wasn't subtle. But the rich man didn't see because he refused to look and ignored God's self-revelation in Moses and the Prophets because his heart was hard, selfish, and cold. The religious leaders listening on got the message! This isn't only a story about compassion for those who suffer; it's a story about faithfulness to God's ways, nature, and revelations.

This parable names what modern societies too often ignore: the vast, growing distance between comfort and poverty and the spiritual danger of insulation. Discipleship isn't just about private holiness. It's about noticing who lies at our gates and responding. It's about how we spend, how we live, and who we include at our tables. It's about taking God's concern for the broken, marginalized, and suffering seriously and being faithful to the Law, Prophets, and Jesus Christ.

Jesus ends with a chilling note. The man begs that Lazarus be sent to warn his brothers. But the reply comes: They have Moses and the prophets. Let them listen. Not even resurrection will convince us if we don't believe the call to justice, mercy, and love already written into God's story.

And here's the sting: Jesus has risen. The warning has come. The invitation still stands. But so does the responsibility. Will you be a person of compassion? Will you be faithful to God's revelations in the Bible? Will you practice the way of Jesus: humility, hospitality, righteousness, mercy, justice, and love?

**Guiding Truth:** Eternal life is shaped by how we respond to suffering now: true discipleship always sees the one at the gate and dares to act.

**Reflection:** Who lies unnoticed at the gate of my comfort, community, or privilege? What does living in light of the great reversal Jesus proclaims mean for me?

**Prayer:** God of compassion, open my eyes to the ones I've ignored. Break my indifference. Teach me to live generously, to love boldly, and to welcome those you call by name. Amen.

# Day 29: Faith, Forgiveness, and the Grateful Stranger

## Reading: Luke 17:1–19

Jesus speaks words that unsettle and remake. "Things that cause people to stumble are bound to come" (v. 1). Woe to the one who becomes the stumbling block. In a world marked by injury, betrayal, and unspoken wounds, Jesus names the reality and then calls his followers to the audacious work of forgiveness. "If another sins and repents—even seven times a day—forgive" (v. 4). Don't tolerate. Don't ignore. Forgive.

Stunned by that command's weight, the disciples plead, "Increase our faith!" (v. 5). But Jesus responds with a paradox: "If you had faith the size of a mustard seed . . ." (v. 6). The issue isn't quantity; it's trust. Faith isn't the power to control, but the willingness to obey, especially when it's hard, when it involves letting go of resentment, releasing what we think we're owed, and beginning again.

Jesus then offers an image of a servant doing their work, not expecting applause but fulfilling duty. The kingdom isn't transactional. It's formed in humility, in doing the good God calls us to do: not for praise, but because love compels it.

Then comes the healing of the ten lepers. Ten cry out. Jesus cleanses ten. But only one returns. And that one is a Samaritan, a stranger, and a religious outsider. He throws himself at Jesus's feet, praising with a full heart. Jesus wonders aloud: "Where are the other nine?" (v. 17). The question echoes through time. So much healing. So little thanks.

Gratitude is more than manners; it's recognition. It's seeing the Giver, not just the gift. It's the posture of a soul that knows it lives by mercy.

This passage invites us to forgive when it feels impossible, to live humbly without applause, and to return to Jesus with the kind of gratitude that falls at his feet.

Forgiveness isn't sentimental; it's revolutionary. To forgive seven times a day is to declare war on bitterness, to resist the violence of vengeance, to believe that grace can interrupt the cycle of harm, and to practice a radical, countercultural lifestyle, in the Way of Jesus. And gratitude? It's not a polite thank-you. It's a cry of recognition, a posture of rebellion in a world that trains us to consume and move on. One turned back. One remembered mercy. One worshiped. In a culture addicted to self-justification, this text calls us to live differently: to forgive relentlessly, to serve quietly, and to return wholeheartedly. The healed are many, but the grateful are few.

**Guiding Truth:** The way of Jesus calls us to live with deep humility, courageous forgiveness, and a faith that returns in gratitude for mercy received.

**Reflection:** Who must I forgive, even if they repeatedly ask? How can I cultivate a deeper habit of gratitude in response to God's healing work in my life?

**Prayer:** Jesus, give me the courage to forgive, the humility to serve, and the clarity to return to you with gratitude. May my life echo with thanks and my faith grow through trust. Amen.

# Day 30: The Kingdom That Comes Quietly

The Pharisees ask Jesus when the kingdom of God will come, expecting perhaps a dramatic uprising or political transformation. But Jesus says, "The kingdom of God is within you" or "in your midst." It's not something to track like a storm system on a radar. It's already here: surprising, countercultural, upside-down, and subversive. He warns the disciples not to chase after signs or run to wilderness prophets. Instead, they should recognize the in-breaking of God's reign already among them.

Then Jesus speaks of suddenness: like lightning, Noah's day, and Lot's escape. The arrival of the Son of Humanity isn't something you schedule or prepare for at leisure. It requires readiness. Don't look back, he says, like Lot's wife did. Remember her. Be present in this moment. Be ready to lose everything if you must.

This passage shakes up spiritual complacency. It's not about deciphering end-times puzzles. It's about seeing the hidden kingdom that quietly disrupts our allegiance to comfort, security, and control. It's about surrendering now, not someday. We want spectacle; God offers incarnation. We want timelines; God offers presence.

Spiritually, this passage invites us to wake up. We're not called to speculate but to live alert, embodied, and anchored in the now. The temptation is to drift into distraction or nostalgia: to look back or forward but not inward. The kingdom doesn't come through panic or calculation. It comes through surrender, through opening our eyes to the presence of Christ among the ordinary.

The kingdom isn't coming with fanfare; it's already brushing up against your skin in the quiet hours, in the aching silence, in the sudden holy hush of ordinary life. If you're always watching the horizon for some grand arrival, you'll miss the whisper in the room you're standing in. The kingdom doesn't compete for attention; it waits, poised in stillness, inviting you to turn aside like Moses at the bush, to notice what you'd otherwise walk past.

The surrender Jesus calls for isn't a dramatic gesture; it's the daily relinquishing of control, the unclenching of fists, and choosing trust over calculation. It's giving up the fantasy of knowing what's next so you can live this moment with holy presence. So, stop scanning the skies. Look inward. Look around. The reign of God isn't coming one day; it's breaking in now, wherever love takes root, wherever grace softens hearts, wherever the cross-shaped way is walked. The apocalyptic isn't always catastrophic. Sometimes, it's just the Spirit slipping in through a cracked-open heart. Wake up. Stay open. The kingdom is already here.

Jesus is clear: his coming will disrupt everything we cling to. Are we ready to lose our lives to find them? Are we living as if the reign of God is at hand, right here, right now?

**Guiding Truth:** The kingdom of God doesn't wait for spectacle; it calls us to surrender in the now.

**Reflection:** Where might you be looking for signs instead of listening for God's quiet voice? What does it mean for you to live ready, not reactive?

**Prayer:** God of the hidden kingdom, awaken me to your presence. Teach me to stop chasing signs and instead live in surrender and attentiveness. Keep my eyes fixed on your reign and my heart ready for your return. Amen.

# Day 31: Crying Out and Coming Low

### Reading: Luke 18:1–14

Jesus tells a story about a persistent widow and an unjust judge. She has no power, money, or influence—just her worn but relentless voice. And she gets justice—not because the judge is good, but because she refuses to be silent. Then Jesus asks: If even an unjust judge responds, how much more will God act for those who cry out day and night?

Then comes another parable: a Pharisee and a tax collector praying in the temple. One boasts; the other pleads. One is full of self; the other empties himself. And it's the broken one who goes home justified.

These two stories belong together. The first teaches bold persistence before God, and the second teaches humble honesty before God. We need both. One cries out with urgency, and the other comes low with surrender. Both are heard.

This passage dismantles two lies. The first is that God doesn't care, and the second is that we can impress God. But here's the truth: God's heart moves toward the desperate and the humble. Crying out isn't weakness: it's faith. Confessing need isn't shameful: it's liberating.

Jesus points us toward a spirituality of both resilience and repentance. We're invited to keep showing up before God, not polished but real. We're asked to stop pretending and just be honest.

There's power in persistence, not because we wear God down, but because our repeated return remakes us. Every cry, every whispered plea, every sigh too deep for words shapes us into people who won't give up on God because we've discovered that God never gives up on us. And humility? It isn't shameful. It's freedom. The tax collector is free precisely because he stops pretending. He stands exposed before God, and he's met with mercy instead of rejection. That's the scandal of grace—it welcomes the raw and unraveled.

Jesus points to the quiet, persevering ones in a world obsessed with image and applause. The ones who don't stop knocking. The ones who fall on their knees instead of flexing their righteousness. These are the people who find the heart of God. So, cry out. Come low. Let prayer make you soft, not slick. Let honesty be your offering. This is the posture Jesus blesses—not performance, not perfection, but broken truthfulness. He hears. He responds. Not because you're eloquent or impressive, but because you're beloved. Come again. Come as you are.

Jesus, the Just One, listens to our cries. He sees the tearful persistence. He honors the tax collector's prayer. He offers not just vindication, but an embrace.

**Guiding Truth:** God welcomes the persistent and the penitent: cry out boldly and come low.

**Reflection:** Are there places where you've stopped crying out because you've grown tired or disillusioned? What mask might you need to remove in prayer this week?

**Prayer:** Listening God, I come again, with my needs and failures. Teach me to pray with boldness and humility. Let my cries rise like incense, and my heart bow in surrender. Meet me in my honesty. Amen.

# Day 32: The Kingdom Belongs to the Childlike

### Reading: Luke 18:15–30

People bring infants to Jesus, and the disciples rebuke them, protecting what they think is the dignity of ministry. But Jesus rebukes the protectors. "Let them come," he says. "The kingdom belongs to such as these." It doesn't belong to the accomplished or the pure: it belongs to the small, the dependent, the overlooked.

Then a ruler approaches. He's moral and successful. "What must I do to inherit eternal life?" he asks. Jesus gently walks him through the commandments but then asks the one thing the man can't give: his wealth. He walks away sad.

These two scenes speak into our divided hearts. We love the idea of childlike faith until it threatens our power, our wealth, our grip on autonomy. But the kingdom doesn't work like the world. It's not achieved. It's received.

Children don't calculate risk. They trust with reckless, open eyes. That's what makes them the perfect picture of kingdom living. They come close with sticky hands and simple hope. They don't bring status; they bring need. That's why Jesus blesses them, not for what they know, but for how they come. But us? We measure. We grasp. We weigh what it will cost. The ruler did too, and he walked away. He had everything, but not what mattered most: a heart free to follow. Jesus doesn't shame him; he grieves for him. Because the door is open, but the man chooses the vault over the kingdom.

This passage pulls the curtain back on our attachments. What are we clutching so tightly that we can't enter freely? Jesus isn't asking us to despise what we have—he's asking if we're willing to release it when it stands in the way of real life. You don't have to be impressive. You just must be available. The kingdom is for those who hold nothing but longing and come running.

Spiritually, this passage invites us to loosen our grip, admit our helplessness, stop bargaining, and surrender. The children are welcomed because they have nothing to prove, while the rich man walks away because he can't bear to lose control.

Jesus points us to a new kind of discipleship: not more achievement but more dependence, not power but vulnerability, not accumulation but letting go.

The promise is stunning: if we give up, we'll receive a hundredfold. Yes, we'll receive persecution, but also joy, community, and life.

**Guiding Truth:** The kingdom can't be earned or hoarded; it's received by those who come empty-handed.

**Reflection:** Where are you holding onto something tightly that Jesus is asking you to release? What does childlike faith look like for you today?

**Prayer:** Jesus, help me come with empty hands and a soft heart. Loosen my grip on the things that keep me from you. Teach me to trust like a child again. Amen.

# Day 33: Eyes Opened by Mercy

## Reading: Luke 18:31–43

For the third time, Jesus tells his disciples about his suffering, death, and resurrection. But they don't get it. Their spiritual eyes are still shut. Then, the scene shifts to a blind beggar near Jericho. While the disciples see with their eyes but remain spiritually blind, the blind man (Bartimaeus) sees more clearly than anyone. He cries, "Jesus, Son of David, have mercy on me!"

The crowd tries to silence him, but he cries louder, and Jesus stops. Mercy makes Jesus stop. He asks, "What do you want me to do for you?" The man says, "Let me see again." And Jesus heals him: not just his eyes but his soul. The man follows, glorifying God.

There's a holy irony here. The one who's physically blind sees the truth of who Jesus is, while the seeing ones walk in confusion. This passage calls us to a desperate kind of faith; not polished or perfect, just hungry for mercy.

Spiritually, we all live somewhere between blindness and sight. We need courage to name what we can't see. We need mercy to be healed. Jesus asks us the same question: "What do you want me to do for you?" Do we dare answer honestly?

Discipleship isn't about having all the correct answers. It's about crying out when others stay silent. It's about letting Jesus open our eyes repeatedly. Your need doesn't repel him. He's drawn to it.

There's a kind of blindness that's deeper than sight; it's the inability to see what matters most. The disciples couldn't grasp the cross, even as Jesus laid it out plainly. But Bartimaeus, blind to the world, saw the truth of who Jesus was. Sometimes desperation reveals what comfort hides. Mercy opens eyes that textbooks never can. And when Jesus stops—he really stops—it's not efficiency but compassion that governs him. The question he asks isn't rhetorical: "What do you want me to do for you?" It's an invitation to honesty. It's a holy pause, asking us to name our ache aloud. Jesus doesn't just heal bodies; he restores dignity. He doesn't just give sight; he gives belonging.

Discipleship begins with that same cry: "Have mercy!" Not a demand, but a declaration of dependence. And mercy flows to those who risk shouting above the crowd, asking when others stay silent, and believing that grace still walks by on dusty roads and listens. Don't hush your need. Let it rise. It might be the clearest prayer you've ever prayed.

**Guiding Truth:** The way to sight begins with a cry for mercy—and the courage to name your need.

**Reflection:** What area of your life feels like spiritual blindness? Are you willing to cry out when others stay quiet?

**Prayer:** Merciful Christ, I need your healing touch. I want to see it again. Please open my eyes to your presence and truth. I won't be silent: have mercy on me. Amen.

# Day 34: Small Men, Big Grace, and Real Accountability

## Reading: Luke 19:1–27

Zacchaeus is a chief tax collector—small in stature but towering in shame. He climbs a tree to catch a glimpse of Jesus. And Jesus stops. "Come down," he says. "I must stay at your house today." The crowd murmurs. Grace offends them.

But Zacchaeus responds with generosity. "I'll give half to the poor. I'll repay four times what I've stolen." Jesus doesn't command this: grace evokes it. "Salvation has come to this house," Jesus says.

Then, he tells a parable about ten servants and a nobleman who entrusts them with minas. Some invest, and one hides the money. When the king returns, he holds them accountable. Faithfulness and fruitfulness matter.

These scenes show grace and stewardship dancing together. Zacchaeus receives mercy and responds with radical generosity. The servants receive trust and are judged on their use of it. Grace doesn't cancel responsibility; it empowers it.

This is about how we live under Christ's reign. It's about what we do with what we're given. Mercy doesn't excuse passivity; it calls forth boldness. The kingdom isn't just received with joy; it's carried with care.

Jesus invites us to climb down from whatever tree we're perched on (shame, fear, curiosity) and join him in the house of grace. But he also invites us to live like stewards: entrusted, responsible, free.

Zacchaeus wasn't just short; he was stuck in a life shaped by greed, rejection, and regret. But he climbed a tree for a glimpse, and Jesus stopped for more than a glance. That's grace: it finds you perched in hiding and invites you to dinner. But grace doesn't leave us where it found us. It stirs something fierce and beautiful inside, a longing to set things right. Zacchaeus doesn't just say sorry. He transforms. And in that moment, he becomes more than a forgiven man; he becomes a steward of redemption.

The following parable shows us what that looks like: we're entrusted with something holy. Not just money, but mercy. Not just talent, but time. We can bury it or multiply it. But either way, we're accountable. Jesus isn't calling us to fear-driven striving. He's inviting us into courageous faithfulness. What will we do with what we've been given? How will we live in light of the visitations of grace? Your life is a mina. Invest it with love.

**Guiding Truth:** Grace invites us to receive mercy and bless God's gifts boldly.

**Reflection:** What part of you needs to come down and receive Jesus' invitation today? What gift have you buried that God's inviting you to invest with love?

**Prayer:** Jesus, come to my house today. Call me down from my hiding place. Let your grace awaken generosity and faithfulness in me. Amen.

# Day 35: Weeping Over What Could Be

### Reading: Luke 19:28–48

Jesus enters Jerusalem on a colt. The crowds cheer. They lay cloaks on the road. They shout blessings. But Jesus is weeping. While others celebrate, he sobs. Why? Because they don't understand what makes for peace. They're looking for power, not presence. They want a warrior, not a servant.

He enters the Temple and drives out those who've turned it into a marketplace. "My house is a house of prayer," he says, "but you've made it a den of robbers." Jesus isn't just angry: he's heartbroken. The Temple was meant to be a sacred meeting place, not a monument to profit.

This is a portrait of a weeping Messiah: a Christ who loves fiercely, enters vulnerably, and disrupts anything that obstructs communion with God. It's a warning against a religion that becomes transactional, against worship that forgets justice, and against spiritual celebration that ignores Christ's heart.

Jesus doesn't just want admiration: he wants transformation. He doesn't call us to cheer from the sidelines but to weep over what's broken and join him in clearing space for the holy.

Spiritually, this passage challenges us to ask: Do we want the kind of peace Jesus brings? Are we willing to let him disrupt our comfort, cleanse our hearts, and call us into prayerful, courageous presence?

Jesus weeps, not because he's weak, but because he loves with a heart unguarded. His tears aren't manipulation; they're lament. They're the ache of what could've been. This isn't sentimentality. It's prophetic sorrow. The kind that sees potential wasted and peace ignored. While the crowds shout praise, Jesus sobs for the blindness beneath the noise. He knows how easily worship can become theater, how quickly temples can be turned into markets, how subtly holiness gets traded for hustle. His cleansing of the temple isn't rage; it's heartbreak. It's the grief of a lover watching covenant become commerce. And still, he comes. Still, he teaches. Still, he offers himself.

Jesus calls us to let go of religion as performance and embrace faith as surrender. So, let his tears become ours. Let his lament cleanse our inner sanctuaries. Let him disturb the false peace we've settled for and replace it with the fierce, holy peace of presence. There's no revival without cleansing. No transformation without tears.

**Guiding Truth:** Jesus weeps over our misunderstanding of peace and calls us to let him cleanse and claim the places of our worship.

**Reflection:** Where has your spiritual life become more performance than prayer? What tables might Jesus need to overturn in you?

**Prayer:** Christ, I welcome your tears. Cleanse what's corrupt, overturn what hinders, and teach me the peace that comes through your presence. Amen.

# Day 36: Questions and Authority

**Reading: Luke 20:1–8**

The religious leaders confront Jesus. "Who gave you this authority?" they demand. But Jesus replies with his question about John the Baptist. They're trapped. If they affirm John, they'll have to accept Jesus. If they deny him, they'll lose the crowd. So, they say, "We don't know." And Jesus says, "Then neither will I tell you."

This moment reveals something more profound than a debate. It's about postures of the heart. The leaders ask a question not to learn, but to trap. Jesus responds not to evade, but to expose their unwillingness to face the truth. He doesn't play their game. He reveals their fear.

Spiritual authority isn't seized: it's revealed through truth, humility, and divine call. Jesus doesn't defend himself like the world defends power. He lives authority. It's rooted in his union with the Father, in his cross-bearing love.

We love questions. They give us the illusion of control. We think if we can ask sharply enough, we can stay safe from surrender. But Jesus doesn't play games with truth. He sees through the smokescreens. His response to the leaders isn't avoidance, it's revelation. He's showing them, and us, that real authority doesn't argue, it lives, breathes, and bleeds. You know it when you see it. And it makes you choose. The question isn't just "Who gave you this authority?" It's "Will I bow to it?" Because Jesus won't force it. He offers it, clothed in cross-bearing love.

The posture he asks of us isn't cleverness, but trust. Not a demand for proof, but an openness to transformation.

Spiritual maturity isn't about having all the right questions. It's about recognizing when the Answer is standing right before you. Don't let defensiveness blind you. Let humility open your heart. And if you must ask questions, let them be the kind that lead to deeper surrender.

This passage reminds us that true authority isn't about title, volume, or control. It's about truth lived, love embodied, and sacrifice embraced. It challenges us to examine our questions: Are we asking to understand or escape? Are we willing to let Jesus's authority shape us?

Jesus doesn't force belief. But he exposes hearts. And he invites us to follow: not because he answers every question, but because he's the answer in flesh.

**Guiding Truth:** Real authority is revealed, not grasped; and it invites humble hearts, not defensive ones.

**Reflection:** When have you used questions to avoid surrender rather than seek truth? What would it mean for Jesus's authority to shape how you live today?

**Prayer:** Jesus, your authority is love and truth. Expose my fear, break my pride, and teach me to follow you not with argument, but with trust. Amen.

# Day 37: The Rejected Stone and the Watching Eyes

### Reading: Luke 20:9–47

Jesus tells a story the religious elite recognize is about them, but they refuse to be changed. A vineyard owner sends servant after servant, then his beloved son, to collect what's due. The tenants beat, shame, and kill. The message is sharp: God has sent prophets, now the Son, and still you resist.

This parable names the deep resistance of religious and political systems to prophetic truth. We can wrap ourselves in Scripture, liturgy, and tradition and still crucify the presence of God when it threatens our control.

When Jesus finishes, the leaders try to trap him with questions about taxes and resurrection. But he doesn't play their game. He reveals that what they think they know (about Scripture, authority, and power) is shallow. God isn't the God of the dead but of the living. Jesus isn't merely a rabbi; he is the rejected stone that has become the cornerstone.

The tension in this passage isn't abstract; it pulses through every generation. The prophets don't come with polished sermons but with dangerous questions. They ask us to name our idols, to confront our complicity, to tear down the false altars we've erected in God's name. And like the tenants, we often respond with dismissal or rage. We silence the voices that disturb our comfort. We ridicule the messengers who refuse to flatter our egos or affirm our control.

But Jesus isn't merely telling a parable about others: he's holding up a mirror. The vineyard is our heart, our church, our nation, our system. The messengers are those experiencing poverty, diplacement, persecution, and intimidation, as well as the whistleblower, the truth-teller, and the inconvenient prophet. And the Son still stands at the gate, asking: will you receive me or reject me again?

This is the Jesus who will not be domesticated. He exposes the corruption beneath our religious polish and still dares to call us beloved. His truth isn't tame, but it's healing. The cornerstone crushes our illusions so that something new can be built: not a temple of fear but a dwelling of mercy, justice, and life.

This passage invites us to self-examination. Where are we protecting our vineyards (our institutions, reputations, ideologies) at the expense of receiving Christ as he really is? It calls us to humility before mystery, to faithfulness over performance, and to a posture of listening rather than defensiveness.

Jesus finishes by warning about leaders who love titles and honor but devour the vulnerable. Empire religion always wears robes. But the kingdom comes clothed in humility.

**Guiding Truth:** God's presence often comes in ways that threaten our sense of power; to receive Jesus is to surrender control and welcome the truth.

**Reflection:** Where might I be resisting Christ in the name of protecting what's mine? What does it look like to build my life on the cornerstone and not the temple of my own making?

**Prayer:** Christ, Cornerstone, break through my resistance. Dismantle my pride. Make me a vessel of truth, not performance: a heart that yields to your prophets, your Word, and your Way. Amen.

# Day 38: The Hidden Wealth of the Widow

## Reading: Luke 21:1–4

While the temple bustles with offerings, Jesus notices a widow. She drops two copper coins: everything she has. No fanfare. No status. But Jesus says she's given more than all the rest.

This isn't just a stewardship lesson. It's a rebuke of systems that allow religious elites to live in excess while people experiencing poverty give all they have. It's a spotlight on the disparity between appearance and reality, between external devotion and internal surrender.

Jesus doesn't criticize her for giving. He honors her faith. But his eyes are on the structure that consumes her life and still demands more. He sees both her sacrifice and the injustice wrapped in ritual.

It's easy to read this story and rush past it as though it's a charming footnote in the Gospel, a brief nod to humble piety. However, this widow's act is profound in its implications. She has no power, no voice, no platform, and yet she offers all she has, not to earn divine favor but because something in her trusts that her giving matters. And Jesus sees her.

To be seen by Jesus is no small thing. In a system where temple leaders are adorned in wealth and power, he notices the one no one else does. He names her gift "more" not because of its market value but because it reveals a heart free from greed and rich in faith. This woman becomes a living parable: the kind of disciple Jesus longs for, the type of courage that kingdom faith requires.

This story raises haunting questions about what we celebrate. Do we see people like this widow? Do our communities honor the quiet givers, the faithful servants, the ones holding everything together behind the scenes? Or do we only notice wealth when it's loud, generosity when it's public, faith when it's platformed?

In a world obsessed with image, measurable impact, and external piety, this text asks us: What is costly worship? What does generosity look like when no one is watching? And what religious systems do we still uphold that leave people experiencing poverty with no choice but to give out of desperation?

This story reminds us that heaven's scales weigh differently. God sees the hidden, honors the small, and isn't impressed by the performance of the powerful.

**Guiding Truth:** True worship costs something, and God sees the offering hidden from the crowd.

**Reflection:** What kind of giving (of my resources, time, or love) comes from trust rather than surplus? Are there systems I'm part of that exploit the devotion of the vulnerable?

**Prayer:** God, who sees the unseen, teaches me to give not out of pride but out of love. Help me honor those whose sacrifices go unnoticed. Shape my life into an offering poured out for you. Amen.

# Day 39: The End of Illusions

## Reading: Luke 21:5–38

As the disciples marvel at the beauty of the temple, Jesus tells them: Not one stone will be left upon another. It's a shock. The temple is the center of worship, power, and national identity. But Jesus sees through the marble and gold to the violence and pride underneath.

He warns of false messiahs, wars, earthquakes, and persecution. It sounds terrifying, but Jesus calls his disciples to a different posture: not fear, but faithfulness. Don't be deceived. Don't be afraid. Stand firm.

This passage has often been misused to stoke fear or justify apocalyptic predictions. But Jesus isn't giving a timetable; he's forming resilient disciples. In times of upheaval, it's easy to be consumed by panic or retreat into denial. But Jesus calls us to be people of presence, people of witness.

Jesus isn't trying to scare us into submission; he's waking us up to reality. The shaking of the world isn't a sign of divine absence but of divine unveiling. False saviors will always offer control, clarity, and escape. But Jesus offers presence, perseverance, and truth. His way doesn't bypass suffering; it walks through it with integrity.

We live in an age that constantly trades in fear. Political voices weaponize anxiety. Religious leaders sometimes profit from panic. But the way of Christ resists the siren song of alarmism. Faithfulness isn't frantic. It's rooted. It's slow. It endures.

Jesus speaks about betrayal, hardship, and even martyrdom: not to discourage but to prepare. Because discipleship was never about survival; it's about witness. In a crisis, we don't merely endure; we testify. Our posture in the storm is itself a message: that hope is stronger than despair, that love endures, that the falling stones of temporary empires do not shake the kingdom.

To follow Jesus in a trembling world isn't to chase certainty but to cling to the One who will never leave, even when the skies darken and the ground shifts beneath our feet.

He promises that not a hair of our heads will perish. That's not a promise of safety but of ultimate belonging. God will hold us. Even in destruction, loss, and persecution, God is nearby.

Jesus ends by telling us to stay awake. Don't get drunk on distraction. Don't let the weight of life pull you under. Pray. Watch. Stand.

The temple will fall. Empires will tremble. But the kingdom remains.

**Guiding Truth:** In a world of instability, Jesus calls us to alertness, courage, and faithfulness, not fear.

**Reflection:** What false securities am I tempted to trust more than Christ's presence? What does spiritual watchfulness look like in the rhythms of my daily life?

**Prayer:** Jesus, my Refuge, teach me to live alert and anchored in you. Shake loose my illusions. Root me in hope, even when the world around me is trembling. Keep me awake to your presence. Amen.

# Day 40: The Price of Betrayal

## Reading: Luke 22:1–6

The Passover approaches. The city is electric with tradition, remembrance, and the smell of sacrifice. And in the shadows, betrayal is quietly bought and sold.

The chief priests, guardians of sacred memory, plot murder. Judas, one of the Twelve (one who walked, ate, and laughed with Jesus), makes a deal. The cost? A pocketful of silver. The method? A private signal in a crowded place. The result? The collision of power, secrecy, and self-interest.

We often imagine betrayal as obvious: cold-hearted or violent. But Luke shows us how betrayal can wear the face of friendship. Judas doesn't rage. He slips away. He looks for an opportunity "when no crowd was present."

This is betrayal by calculation, not passion. It's a betrayal that waits for the quiet moment, the hidden deal. And it's not just Judas. Religious systems join hands with the empire. Faith gets weaponized for control. The sacred gets sold for power.

Betrayal rarely begins in a moment. It starts in the slow erosion of trust, in the quiet spaces where fear grows louder than love. Judas didn't suddenly turn. He slid. Step by step. Doubt by doubt. It might've started when Jesus praised someone else. Or when he spoke of suffering instead of victory. Or when the dream of power gave way to talk of crosses and death.

That's what makes betrayal so dangerous: it can grow in silence. We don't always notice when our devotion turns into resentment when our loyalty calcifies into disillusionment. We say the right things. We stay close to Jesus. But our hearts have already begun to drift.

And in a culture addicted to success, image, and self-protection, we're all vulnerable. We want a Jesus who guarantees comfort, who avoids conflict, who plays by the rules of empire. But the real Jesus breaks all of that. He upends tables. He forgives enemies. He walks toward suffering.

If we're honest, there are parts of us that want to manage Jesus rather than follow him. But he won't be managed. He can only be loved or betrayed.

Luke tells us Satan entered Judas, but not as a possession, as seduction. He was already near the edge. The invitation was already whispering: you could secure your future. You could control the story. You could avoid the scandal of the cross.

And maybe that's the haunting part. Betrayal doesn't begin with silver. It starts with disillusionment, self-protection, and a sense of entitlement. It begins when we start to believe Jesus should be someone other than who he is.

This short passage asks us: Where have we made quiet deals with systems of violence or manipulation? Where do we look for "opportune moments" to serve ourselves while still wearing the name of disciple?

**Guiding Truth:** Betrayal often begins not with silver but with self-preservation dressed in the guise of religion.

**Reflection:** In what subtle ways am I tempted to control Jesus rather than follow him? Where have I sold out grace for the sake of comfort or security?

**Prayer:** Jesus, keep me from the slow drift toward betrayal. Please give me the courage to follow you when it costs me. Expose my secret deals and lead me back to the table of mercy. Amen.

# Day 41: The Table and the Sword

## Reading: Luke 22:7–38

Jesus sends Peter and John to prepare for Passover. It's a sacred meal, loaded with memory: liberation from Egypt, the blood on the doorposts, the God who saves. But Jesus reframes it: "This is my body . . . this is my blood."

At this table, he gives not just bread and wine but himself. The center of salvation is no longer a lamb on a doorframe but a Savior who will be broken and poured out.

And yet, even at this table of grace, the disciples argue about greatness. Jesus has just spoken of betrayal and sacrifice, and they debate rank. It's so human it aches. The kingdom is breaking in, and they're still playing empire games.

Jesus doesn't rage. He re-teaches. "The greatest among you must become like the youngest . . . I am among you as one who serves."

Then he looks at Peter. "Satan has asked to sift you like wheat . . . but I have prayed for you." Jesus sees the failure coming. And he's already praying through it.

Peter insists he'll never fall away. But Jesus knows. Still, he entrusts Peter with a future: "When you return, strengthen your siblings." Not if. When.

Finally, Jesus speaks of swords. It's a cryptic moment. The disciples misunderstand, and Jesus ends the discussion: "That's enough."

Because they still don't see. This isn't a battle won by blades. It's a kingdom of cross, not conquest.

Jesus speaks of swords not to incite violence but to expose misunderstanding. The disciples are still imagining a kingdom that will rise by force, defend its borders, and punish its enemies. But Jesus is preparing them for a different kind of struggle: a spiritual sifting, an inner warfare that won't be won by steel but by surrender. They carry literal blades while missing the spiritual danger right in front of them: pride, fear, betrayal, and self-deception.

This is how we often fight. We sharpen our arguments, posture with certainty, and prepare to win the world with strength. But Jesus says, That's enough. Not because the danger isn't real but because the method is wrong. He's not raising warriors of dominance but servants who bleed love into broken places. The battle isn't won with violence. It's won with a cross, a towel, and a table.

This entire passage is filled with tension: love and fear, loyalty and denial, sacred memory, and the prospect of future betrayal. Jesus holds it all. He feeds the denier, includes the ambitious, and prays for the failing.

This is our Lord. This is our table.

**Guiding Truth:** Jesus offers his body to us even when we bring betrayal, confusion, and pride to the table.

**Reflection:** What do I bring to the table: fear, ambition, doubt? Can I let Jesus meet me there? Who is Jesus calling me to strengthen, even in the wake of my weakness?

**Prayer:** Christ of the table, you feed me even when I'm confused, prideful, or afraid. Let your mercy reframe my memory and shape my future. Make me one who serves and one who returns to strengthen others. Amen.

# Day 42: The Cup and the Crushing

## Reading: Luke 22:39–46

Jesus leaves the upper room and walks to the Mount of Olives. It's familiar ground. It's where he taught, prayed, wept. And now, it's where he'll sweat blood.

He tells the disciples, "Pray that you may not enter into temptation." Then he walks a stone's throw away and collapses into agony.

This isn't a serene surrender. This is crushing grief. "Father, if you are willing, remove this cup from me." The cup isn't merely death; it's the full weight of sin, violence, betrayal, and shame. It's drinking the worst of humanity and absorbing it into grace.

We often rush to the cross, bypassing the garden. But the garden is where most of our battles are fought. Not in public trials but in private agonies. In the moments when surrender feels like death and silence seems like abandonment. The cup Jesus faces is personal. It's not abstract suffering; it's betrayal by friends, injustice by the powerful, and the abandonment of all who once claimed to love him.

We know this garden, too. The place where obedience feels unbearable. Where we plead for another way. Where we bargain, tremble, question. And yet, Jesus doesn't run. He stays. He prays. He cries blood into the dirt. His faith isn't sanitized. It's wrung out of anguish. This is what courage looks like: not the absence of sorrow, but trust that holds steady in its grip.

What if Gethsemane isn't just Jesus's agony but our invitation?

And yet: "Not my will, but yours be done." This is the holy pivot. The surrender that breaks the world open. The obedience that births salvation.

An angel strengthens him. But still, the sorrow doesn't lift. He prays more earnestly. His sweat becomes blood. Luke, ever the physician, records the physical toll of spiritual suffering.

Meanwhile, the disciples sleep. Not out of laziness but exhaustion. "They were sleeping because of grief." Grief can wear you down until even prayer feels impossible.

Jesus returns, wakes them, and asks: "Why are you sleeping?" It's not condemnation. It's a call. "Pray that you may not enter into temptation."

This passage is the still point in the storm. Jesus chooses the cross before anyone lays a hand on him. This is where redemption begins: in a dark garden, with a whispered yes.

**Guiding Truth:** Before Jesus bore the cross on his shoulders, he bore the cost in his will.

**Reflection:** What cup have I been avoiding? Where is God calling me to surrender in trust, not fear? What does watchful, prayerful discipleship look like in a weary world?

**Prayer:** Jesus, in the garden of agony, you chose love. Help me say yes to the path before me. Strengthen me in my grief. Keep me watchful and surrendered, even when I'm weary. Your will, not mine. Amen.

# Day 43: The Rooster, the Fire, and the Eyes of Christ

### Reading: Luke 22:47–71

The quiet garden is shattered. Judas steps forward, not with a sword, but with a kiss. His betrayal is intimate, camouflaged in affection. And still, Jesus doesn't pull back. He names the moment: "Judas, are you betraying the Son of Man with a kiss?" It's not a rebuke; it's heartbreak.

The disciples lash out. One cuts off an ear. But Jesus stops the violence. He heals the wound. In the face of betrayal and arrest, Jesus chooses mercy.

Then Peter follows at a distance: close enough to see but far enough to feel safe. Around a fire in the courtyard, the denials begin. Three times, he's asked. Three times, he insists, "I don't know him." The third time, the rooster crows.

And then: "The Lord turned and looked at Peter." That line breaks my heart. Jesus, arrested, beaten, and betrayed, turns and meets Peter's eyes. Not with condemnation. With love. With knowing. With sorrow and mercy.

Peter weeps bitterly. It's the cry of a heart that knows it's broken trust but hasn't lost hope. Because even in failure, he's still seen.

There's a sacredness in this look: Jesus meeting Peter in the very moment of collapse. It's not a glare of shame. It's a gaze that holds both grief and grace. Peter sees in Jesus's eyes what we all need to see in our lowest moment: you aren't discarded. Even as Peter disowns Jesus with his lips, Jesus refuses to disown Peter with his eyes.

This is what redemption begins to look like: not after we've fixed everything, but right in the wreckage. Jesus doesn't need Peter to get it right before looking at him. The love comes first. The look comes first. That's how transformation works: not as a reward for strength but as mercy in our undoing.

And that look is still searching for us at the fires of our compromise, in the echoes of our denials, amid the grief we try to hide.

Jesus is mocked, blindfolded, beaten. His identity is questioned; his face is struck. "Prophesy! Who hit you?" they sneer. Ironically, he already had.

Before the council, Jesus speaks only enough. "If I tell you, you will not believe. . . . but from now on, the Son of Man will be seated at the right hand of power." They hear blasphemy. But it's truth wrapped in restraint.

This whole passage is about presence: betraying presence, distant presence, merciful presence, prophetic presence. Jesus remains who he is, even as everyone else falters.

**Guiding Truth:** Even in our denial and weakness, Jesus meets us with mercy, not rejection.

**Reflection:** Where am I following Jesus at a distance, hoping to stay safe? What might Jesus's eyes be saying to me right now in my failure or fear?

**Prayer:** Christ of the courtyard and the cross, turn and meet my eyes, not in wrath, but in love. I've denied you with my fear, but I long to return. Let my tears become transformation. Amen.

# Day 44: A Silence That Judges Power

## Reading: Luke 23:1–25

Jesus is handed over to Pilate—the accusations swirl: subversion, tax refusal, false claims of kingship. But Pilate finds no guilt. Nor does Herod. Still, the machinery of the empire keeps turning. Power must be appeased. Crowds must be calmed. Innocence is inconvenient.

Pilate sends Jesus to Herod. Herod mocks him, clothes him in royal garb, and sends him back. He's entertainment to some, a threat to others, but a king to almost no one.

Through it all, Jesus barely speaks. His silence isn't cowardice; it's judgment. It exposes the emptiness of empire and the fear behind power.

Something is unsettling about the quiet. In a scene dominated by noise (accusations, political maneuvering, jeering crowds), Jesus refuses to participate in the spectacle. His silence speaks louder than words. It isn't passive. It's prophetic. In a world where every leader must assert control and every voice clamors to be heard, Jesus stands still, exposing the hollow performances of those who claim authority.

This is the kind of power that unnerves both Rome and religion: a power not rooted in coercion or control but in self-giving love. His stillness unravels their certainty. His composure disarms their posturing. Jesus doesn't plead for release or lash out in anger. He doesn't need to. His silence is a mirror, reflecting cowardice, corruption, and complicity.

And in that silence, we're forced to ask: when faced with injustice, do we shout, flee, or stand in the stillness of Christ?

Then comes the choice: Barabbas or Jesus? A violent insurrectionist or the Prince of Peace? The people choose Barabbas. Always Barabbas. Because the empire would rather have a weapon than a cross. It understands force but fears grace.

Pilate wants to release Jesus. He says so three times. But the crowd, incited by leaders, cries, "Crucify him!" louder and louder. And in the end, Pilate gives in, not to justice, but to pressure. He releases the guilty and condemns the innocent.

This passage names our culture's addiction to violence, the ease with which we scapegoat, and the danger of leaders without courage. But it also shows Jesus choosing love in the face of rejection, truth in the face of lies, and silence in the face of noise.

He is the rejected King. And he still walks into our verdicts with dignity.

**Guiding Truth:** When the world chooses Barabbas, Jesus still chooses the cross.

**Reflection:** Where am I tempted to appease the crowd rather than stand for what's right? In what ways have I underestimated the cost of grace?

**Prayer:** King of truth and mercy, give me the courage to stand with you when the crowd turns away. Teach me to value justice more than popularity. And help me see the silent strength of your love. Amen.

# Day 45: The Crucified King and the Crucified Thief

## Reading: Luke 23:26–43

Jesus is led away. He stumbles under the weight of the cross, and Simon of Cyrene is pulled from the crowd to carry it. An involuntary disciple. A stranger caught in grace.

Women weep as Jesus passes, but he tells them: "Don't weep for me. Weep for yourselves." It's a haunting line. Even on the road to death, he's thinking of others. Warning of judgment. Grieving what's to come.

He's crucified between two criminals. On either side, suffering. On either side, the cross. One mocks. One pleads: "Remember me." And Jesus, in agony, responds: "Today you will be with me in paradise."

This is the scandal of grace: a thief condemned by society, welcomed by heaven. No good works. No theology. Just surrender. And Jesus, crowned in thorns, becomes his king.

The thief doesn't clean himself up. He doesn't recite doctrine. He doesn't promise reform. He simply turns toward Jesus in vulnerability and asks to be remembered. That's what faith looks like when there's no time to prove anything. And Jesus responds, not with conditions, but with immediacy: Today. Not after purgatory. Not after a probationary period. Today, paradise.

This isn't a theology of cheap grace; it's a vision of costly mercy. The thief isn't rescued from the consequences of his life, but he is rescued from despair. And that's what Jesus does: he makes holy the very places we thought were beyond redemption. He turns death itself into a doorway.

In a world that demands credentials, performance, and purity, this moment dismantles every ladder we try to climb. Salvation isn't earned; it's received. The only thing the thief brings is need. And apparently, that's enough for Jesus to call him "with me."

The sign over the cross reads, "This is the King of the Jews." It's meant to mock. But it's true. Not despite the cross but through it.

This isn't a sentimental story. It's a confrontation. The cross exposes our violence, our systems, and our saviors, who are made in our image. And Jesus remains: forgiving, embracing, reigning from wood and nails.

This passage asks us to choose again: Which thief am I? Which king do I follow?

**Guiding Truth:** Jesus reigns not from a throne but from a cross, and paradise is offered to the broken.

**Reflection:** What part of me still mocks the way of the cross, seeking a more "sensible" salvation? Where am I being invited to surrender, like the thief who was remembered?

**Prayer:** Jesus, crucified and crowned, remember me. Not because I am worthy, but because you are love. In my weakness, meet me with paradise. In my fear, speak forgiveness. Let your cross become the place where my heart bows. Amen.

# Day 46: The Shattered Veil and the Silent Tomb

### Reading: Luke 23:44–56

Darkness falls at midday. Not metaphor but reality. A thick, aching sky wraps the world in grief. Creation itself groans as if in labor. Something cosmic is breaking, something ancient being undone. At the center of it all is a cross and the One who hangs there.

In the temple, the curtain (thick, woven, and holy) tears from top to bottom. Not from the ground up, as if by human effort, but from heaven downward. It's not just fabric ripping. It's separation being undone. The veil that kept people at a distance from the Most Holy Place is torn apart by mercy. What religion once guarded with fear, Jesus opens with flesh and love.

Jesus cries out, not in despair, but in power. "Father, into your hands, I commit my spirit." This isn't resignation. It's a regal surrender. A sovereign laying down his life on his terms. In this cry, death is dethroned. The powers of fear and exclusion are unseated. The final breath of Jesus breathes new air into a suffocating world.

And it's not the insiders who first recognize what's happening. It's a centurion, an agent of empire, trained in the art of death. He watches how Jesus dies and says, "Surely this was a righteous man." It's a declaration drenched in wonder. A confession from the margins. Grace, it seems, begins to bloom in the most unexpected places.

Meanwhile, the women who followed Jesus from Galilee stand at a distance. They say nothing. They don't leave. They watch. Their witness is wordless but not unnoticed. Sometimes, faith looks like staying near to what breaks your heart.

Then comes Joseph of Arimathea, a quiet disciple, a council member, a man of courage hidden in restraint. He goes to Pilate. He asks for the body. He offers his tomb. In a world where power rushes to cover shame, Joseph honors it. He wraps the body in linen and lays it gently on a rock. He refuses to let violence and empire dictate the final act. His devotion is a defiant tenderness.

The women follow even here. They watch where he is laid. Then they go home and prepare spices. Love isn't finished yet. Even in death, they are ready to serve.

This is where resurrection begins: not with spectacle, but with silence. Not with clarity but with courage. In the dark space between the cross and the dawn, we are invited to wait and believe that God isn't done. Hope is buried, but only for a time. Heaven's plan now rests in borrowed space. The veil is torn, but the story still waits to rise.

Sometimes, the most potent acts of faith look like wrapping the broken body of hope, walking home in grief, and still preparing the spices.

**Guiding Truth:** The death of Jesus tears down every barrier between God and us and calls us to courage in the silence.

**Reflection:** What veils in my life still hide God's nearness? Where is God calling me to quiet courage in a time of apparent defeat?

**Prayer:** Jesus, torn for us, draw me beyond the veil. Teach me to stand with the grieving, to honor your body in the silence, and to trust that even in the tomb, you are at work. Let my waiting be worship. Amen.

# Day 47: Fragrance, Fear, and the Empty Place

## Reading: Luke 24:1–12

At dawn, the women arrive: grief pressing down, spices in hand, hearts broken. They don't come expecting joy. They come to anoint a corpse. They do what love does when hope is gone: they show up, not to change the outcome, but to honor the loss. But the body is gone. The stone is rolled back. The tomb is empty.

And then: light. Two radiant figures appear. The air shifts from mourning to mystery. Their question slices through the fog: "Why do you look for the living among the dead?" It's not a rebuke; it's an awakening. A theological earthquake. A call to stop seeking divine life in places shaped by decay, fear, and finality. The question doesn't just belong to the first century; it echoes across every generation. Why do we cling to dead institutions, tired certainties, and hollow identities, expecting life?

The women remember Jesus's words. That's the turning point: not the angels, not even the empty tomb, but the remembering. When grief begins to give way to memory, the resurrection takes root. What Jesus said now blooms with meaning. And suddenly, they're running: not from fear, but with fire. They became the first preachers of resurrection, bearing the gospel before pulpits were built.

They tell the apostles, but their words are dismissed as nonsense. It's too much, too wild, too soon. Resurrection often is. It doesn't obey reason. It doesn't wait for permission. It breaks the logic of despair and reorders reality from the inside out.

Still, Peter runs. He doesn't believe, but he runs. He bends over the tomb and sees linen, not a body. He leaves marveling, caught between loss and wonder. This is the grace of Easter: you don't have to understand to begin. Sometimes, resurrection faith starts not with answers but with movement. Sometimes, all you can do is show up, with disbelief in hand, and marvel.

This story teaches us that resurrection doesn't arrive with trumpets and clarity. It creeps in at dawn. It finds us with spices still clutched in our hands. It confronts our categories, reverses our hierarchies, and calls the silenced to speak. Women become witnesses. The grave becomes the pulpit. Despair becomes a proclamation.

The stone is rolled away, not just from a tomb, but from the hearts that had been sealed by sorrow.

**Guiding Truth:** Resurrection begins where we least expect it: when memory meets mystery and love keeps showing up.

**Reflection:** Where am I still looking for life among the dead? What do I need to remember to recognize resurrection?

**Prayer:** God of the dawn, help me remember what you've said and trust what I cannot yet see. Let me carry the fragrance of hope into places still shadowed by grief. Let your Word stir memory, and your Spirit awaken faith. Amen.

# Day 48: The Stranger on the Road

### Reading: Luke 24:13–35

Two disciples walk away from Jerusalem, away from the whirlwind, the trauma, the dashed hopes. The road to Emmaus isn't just physical; it's emotional. It's the path of disillusionment. They had staked everything on Jesus. And now, they rehearse the pain aloud: "We had hoped…"—perhaps the most devastating phrase in all of Scripture.

And then, Jesus comes. Not in glory, but in anonymity. He joins them as a stranger. He listens before he speaks. He walks before he teaches. This is grace: that Jesus meets us not in the sanctuary of understanding but on the road of sorrow. He doesn't rush their healing. He lets the ache unfold.

Then, he opens the Scriptures. Not to prove a point but to tell the story: his story, threaded through suffering and glory, through the Law, Prophets, and Psalms. But still, they don't see. Knowledge alone doesn't spark recognition. Only communion does.

At the table, he breaks bread. And then (only then) their eyes are opened. Recognition doesn't come in argument but in intimacy. In that familiar act, they remember who he is. And as quickly as he appears, he vanishes. Because he is no longer beside them; he is within them. Their hearts had been burning long before their minds caught up.

And so, they run. Seven miles back into the night. They don't wait for the morning. They return to the very place of their despair with new breath in their lungs. Their sorrow had become a testimony: their defeat, a doorway.

This passage teaches that resurrection meets us on the road of disappointment. That Christ listens to our laments before he gives us light. That Scripture unfolds not as mere instruction but as an invitation. Sometimes, Jesus is closest when we feel most abandoned.

And it reminds us that resurrection isn't just a belief. It's an encounter. A meal. A flame in the chest.

**Guiding Truth:** Jesus meets us on the road of disappointment, opening our eyes not with spectacle but with presence.

**Reflection:** What hopes have I buried that Jesus wants to walk through with me? Where might he be present in what feels ordinary or broken?

**Prayer:** Jesus, stranger and companion, burns in my heart again. Walk beside me in my doubts. Break the bread that opens my eyes. Turn my mourning walk into a witness run. Let me feel the heat of your nearness. Amen.

# Day 49: The Wounds and the Witness

### Reading: Luke 24:36–49

The disciples are huddled in confusion. Reports swirl: an empty tomb, a vision of angels, strangers who claimed to have walked with Jesus. But they are still locked in a room, still prisoners of fear.

And then, Jesus comes. No knock. No warning. Just presence. "Peace be with you." He says it not because the storm is over but because he is the peace amid it.

They are startled. Frightened. They think they're seeing a ghost. But Jesus doesn't shame their fear. He invites their touch. "Look at my hands and my feet." The marks are still there. Resurrection doesn't erase the wounds; it redeems them. His glorified body still carries the memory of suffering.

To prove he's real, he eats. Not because he needs the food but because they need the reassurance. He meets them in the most human of acts: sharing a meal. The sacred slips into the ordinary.

Then, he opens their minds. Scripture, once confused and fragmented, now becomes fire. The Messiah had to suffer, he says. Resurrection isn't a divine detour; it's the beating heart of the story.

And then comes the call: "You are witnesses of these things." Not experts. Not theologians. Witnesses: those who've seen, touched, wept, rejoiced.

But they're not sent empty-handed. Jesus promises power from on high. And so, he tells them: wait. Resurrection gives vision, but

Pentecost gives power. Until then, witness begins in worship, in waiting, in trust.

This passage is a hinge between crucifixion and commission. It shows us that Jesus doesn't rush resurrection faith. He welcomes fear, redeems wounds, shares food, opens minds, and only then sends us out.

We aren't witnesses because we understand everything. We are witnesses because we have been in the room where Jesus came, where fear was real and peace still arrived.

**Guiding Truth:** Jesus sends us out not despite our wounds but through them, bearing witness to peace made real.

**Reflection:** How might Jesus want to use my wounds to witness to others? Where am I being invited to wait for power before stepping out?

**Prayer:** Risen Christ, show me again your wounds and your peace. Send me not in strength but in Spirit. Make me a witness who walks gently, speaks boldly, and lives resurrection daily. Let my waiting be as holy as my going. Amen.

# Day 50: Hands Raised and Heaven Opened

## Reading: Luke 24:50–53

The Gospel of Luke ends not with silence or sorrow but with uplifted hands and a rising Christ. After all the suffering, misunderstandings, grief, fear, and flickers of hope, this is how the story closes: Jesus blessing his disciples as he departs. There are no dramatic farewells. No thunder or veil. Just blessing. Just hands raised in love.

Jesus leads them out to Bethany, a small, familiar place just beyond the city. Not to a throne or temple or seat of empire but to a hillside marked by everyday memory. It's here, amid the ordinary, that heaven opens. He lifts his hands, blesses them, and is carried up. The last image they see of Jesus isn't a cross or a tomb; it's a blessing extended in midair, eternal in gesture and grace.

And they worship. Not the kind of worship that retreats from the world but the kind that burns with joy. They return to Jerusalem not with fear but with great joy: a phrase so unexpected for a farewell. There's no more hiding, no more shame. Their lives, once defined by fear, now overflow with praise.

This final passage reframes absence. Jesus departs, but the disciples don't feel abandoned. The gap between heaven and earth isn't felt as distance but as expansion. They have become witnesses to something uncontainable. Resurrection has not just changed their theology: it's reshaped their imagination, restructured their courage, and lit their hearts on fire.

Luke's gospel begins in the temple with a priest struck silent and ends in the temple with disciples bursting into praise. From silence to song. From law to love. From routine to radical hope. Their worship isn't escapism; it's fuel for mission. They aren't grieving the loss of Jesus. They are bearing the glory of his presence in the world.

This passage reminds us that we are always living between blessing and commissioning. Between hands raised over us and Spirit poured within us, between the memory of his words and the urgency of our witness.

We live in a world thick with noise and illusion, where despair often masquerades as realism and numbness is mistaken for wisdom. But this final vision invites us to live from joy, not shallow optimism, but the deep, defiant joy that flows from knowing Christ has overcome death and that his kingdom is already breaking in.

This joy becomes resistance. Worship becomes witness. And the church (imperfect and ordinary as it is) becomes the place where heaven and earth still meet.

**Guiding Truth:** Even in absence, Jesus blesses and sends us, calling us to live in joyful witness shaped by resurrection hope.

**Reflection:** Where am I being invited to live from blessing rather than fear? How can joy become the foundation of my discipleship and resistance?

**Prayer:** Christ who ascended with blessing still on your lips, lift my heart to praise. Let joy replace fear, and worship become my witness. Make my life echo with your presence, even when I cannot see. Amen.

# Appendix 1: Would You Help?

Writing a book takes immense effort. It's a sustained labor of love over months, even years. Every page carries hours of thought, prayer, revision, and hope. And while the writing may be solitary, the life of a book is communal. That's where you come in. If this book has meant something to you, I'd be deeply grateful if you could help it find its way into more hands and hearts.

There are two simple but powerful ways you can do that.

First, consider leaving a short review on Amazon (and Goodreads would be wonderful too). Even just a few sentences can help others discover the book, as reviews significantly influence how books are recommended and shared online. You can do that by visiting Amazon or searching for this book and writing a review. Even a short note helps people find the book.

Second, if the book has stirred something in you, would you share it with others: friends, groups, churches, or anyone who might benefit from its message?

Your support helps keep this work going, and it means more than I can say. Thank you for being part of this journey.

Find this book on these pages:
1. Amazon:
https://www.amazon.com.au/stores/author/B008NI4ORQ
2. Goodreads:
https://www.goodreads.com/author/show/20347171.Graham_Joseph
_Hill

3. Author Website:

https://grahamjosephhill.com/books/

# Appendix 2: About Me

Graham Joseph Hill (OAM, PhD) is an Adjunct Research Fellow and Associate Professor at Charles Sturt University, and one of Australia's most prolific and awarded Christian authors. He's written more than twenty books, including *Salt, Light, and a City*, which was named Jesus Creed's 2012 Book of the Year (church category); *Healing Our Broken Humanity* (with Grace Ji-Sun Kim), named Outreach Magazine's 2019 Resource of the Year (culture category); and *World Christianity*, shortlisted for the 2025 Australian Christian Book of the Year. In 2024, Graham was awarded the Medal of the Order of Australia (OAM) for his service to theological education. He lives in Sydney with his wife, Shyn.

## Author and Ministry Websites

GrahamJosephHill.com
GrahamJosephHill.Substack.com
youtube.com/@GrahamJosephHill_Author
Linktr.ee/dailydevotions
facebook.com/grahamjosephhill/
instagram.com/grahamjosephhill/
amazon.com.au/stores/author/B008NI4ORQ
goodreads.com/author/show/20347171.Graham_Joseph_Hill

## Books

See all my books at GrahamJosephHill.com/books

# Appendix 3: Connect With Me

I'd love to stay connected with you. You can sign up to my Substack, Spirituality and Society with Hilly, where I share new writing, spiritual reflections, and updates on future books. Please find me on Substack: https://grahamjosephhill.substack.com

You can also find my books on my website: https://grahamjosephhill.com/books

You can also connect with me through my Facebook author page: https://www.facebook.com/GrahamJosephHill/

www.ingramcontent.com/pod-product-compliance
Lightning Source LLC
Chambersburg PA
CBHW031557040426
42452CB00006B/331